Rupert Furneaux is the author of a number of books
published in Britain, the United States, and in translation. He has specialised in the unravelling of famous
mysteries, such as the identity of the Man in the Iron
Mask and the fate of the crew of the drifting ghost
ship, the *Mary Celeste*. At one time or another he has
written about all the famous mysteries, most recently
in *The Ancient Mysteries*. He is now engaged in the
search for Captain Kidd's treasure, having identified
the island depicted in the charts found in the nineteen
thirties. His initial exploration was the subject of a
television programme shown in the summer of 1975.
But, he says, no other mystery can compare with that
of *The Money Pit*.

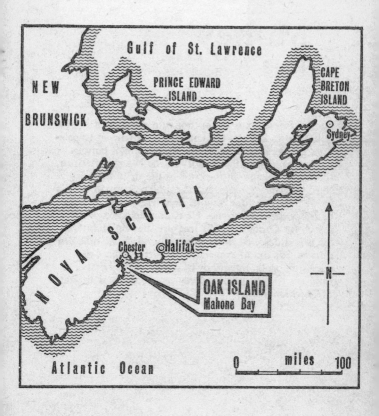

Money Pit
The Mystery of Oak Island

Rupert Furneaux

FONTANA/COLLINS

By the same author MYSTERIES

The Man Behind the Mask
The World's Strangest Mysteries
What Happened on the Mary Celeste
The World's Most Intriguing Mysteries

BATTLES

The Great Siege of Plevna
The Zulu War
Conquest 1066 (In US Invasion 1066)
Saratoga
The Roman Siege of Jerusalem

OTHERS

Massacre at Amritsar
Krakatoa

First published in Great Britain by Tom Stacey Ltd 1972
First published by Fontana 1976

Printed in Canada by Universal Printers Ltd.,
Winnipeg, Manitoba

Copyright © Rupert Furneaux 1972

Contents

APPENDICES

Acknowledgements

I acknowledge with grateful thanks the help given by
these individuals and Institutions:
Brian Backman (skin-diver, 1961); Peter Beamish (visitor to the
island, 1965-6); Gordon Blair (Halifax, N.S.); British
Admiralty Hydrographic Department; Joe Carsley (Chester,
N.S.); M. R. Chappell (soil owner, eastern end of island);
Gordon Coles (Chappell's lawyer, Halifax, N.S.);
L. C. Dalgetty (Division of Geomagnetism Department of
Mines, Ottawa); Robert Dunfield (excavator 1965-6); A. Elgar
(British Embassy, Port-au-Prince, Haiti); Royal Forestry
Society of England and Wales; R. S. Garrett; Robert Gay
(Halifax, N.S.); D. F. Gibbs; Royal Greenwich Observatory
(Herstmonceux, Sussex); John Gwynne-Evans (visitor to island,
1965); Edwin Hamilton (excavator 1941-3); the late R. V.
Harris (Halifax, N.S.); J. H. Haslett; Gilbert Hedden
(excavator 1935); Anthony Howlett (Kidd-Palmer Charts);
W. L. Johnson (investigator and excavator 1958-62); R. A.
Linton; J. E. McCellan; Marine Science Branch of Department
of Mines, Ottawa (coastal erosion); K. W. Merrylees; Colonel
John Montrésor (about his ancestor); National Maritime
Museum (Greenwich); Frederick Nolan (soil owner, middle
section of island); Nova Scotia Provincial Government (Deputy
Provincial Secretaries, C. L. Beazley and H. F. Muggah);
Nova Scotia Public Archives (Dr Bruce Ferguson and Miss
Phyllis Blakeley); J. P. F. O'Connor; Public Record Office,
London (Commander Michael Godfrey and Mr Bell); C.
Raymond (interpreter of cipher); R. Lewis Reynish (adviser
surveying and co-investigator); Miss Gloria Robertson (Institute
of Jamaica); John Rowe (Chief Forester, Stansted Park,
Sussex); Charles Roper and George Bates (surveyors, island
1937); the late R. A. Skelton (Superintendent, Map Room,
British Museum); W. O. Skeat (Institute of Water Engineers);
J. Follows Smith; Southern Carolina Department of Archives
and History; Colonel F. T. Stear (Royal Engineer Historical
Society); C. Stephenson; Colin Summers (visitor to island,

1965); Maurice Taylor (Kidd-Palmer Charts); David Tobias (excavator 1967-71); Professor E. R. Vincent (interpreter of cipher); Alarik Walton; Hilary Watson (my son-in-law). Illustrations: Canadian Department of Mines, 1; John Gwynne-Evans, 2, 5; *Halifax Herald-Chronicle*, 8; Nova Scotia Information Service, 6.

Foreword

The mystery of Oak Island, Nova Scotia, is famous in Canada and the United States, but little known elsewhere. I heard of it in 1939. It intrigued and fascinated me. I visited the island in 1966 and 1967.

For more than one hundred and seventy years hosts of eager treasure hunters have tunnelled and dug in vain attempts to find the immense wealth that is believed to lie in the depths of the Money Pit, as it is appropriately named. More money has been poured into it than is likely to be taken from it.

Imperceptibly, the treasure hunt has evolved into a response to a challenge:
The Money Pit and its impregnable defences excite our curiosity, our desire to conquer the unknown and to disclose its secrets. It is a battle of wits between modern man and the genius who set out to entice and frustrate the trespassers who might stumble upon the bait he dangled before their eyes.

1 Someone Has Been Digging

The story starts in 1795. In the summer of that year sixteen-year-old Daniel McGinnis, a resident of Chester, the small town on the eastern shore of Mahone Bay, went canoeing. He paddled four miles across the bay, landing on a small island close to the western shore. It carried a dense growth of oak trees, unlike the other 360-odd islands in the bay. Why that particular island attracted McGinnis is unknown. He pulled up his boat in a crescent-shaped cove on its south-eastern shore. Either then or later he noticed a large boulder, semi-submerged, in which was affixed a heavy ring-bolt. McGinnis roamed through the trees, following an ancient path up the slope from the beach. The trees thinned out and he found himself walking through a wide clearing in the centre of which stood a gnarled and ancient oak tree. Inspecting the tree, McGinnis saw that, some sixteen ft. or so above ground, a branch had been lopped short. It overhung a depression in the ground. (According to one version of the story, an ancient ship's tackle-block hung from the branch, and its bark was scored by ropes.) In the clearing the first growth of wood had been cut down and another was springing up to take its place. Some old stumps of oak trees were visible. McGinnis also noticed the remains of a tolerably well made road running from north-east to south-west on the island.

His curiosity excited and his thoughts boiling, McGinnis hurried home. He returned to the island next day accompanied by his two friends, John Smith aged twenty, and Anthony Vaughan aged thirteen. The three boys inspected the tree. When one boy climbed up and touched the tackle-block it fell to the ground, shattering into a dozen pieces.

'Someone has been digging,' remarked one boy. 'Digging for what?' asked another. 'For treasure,' suggested the third. 'Or to *bury* treasure,' exclaimed the first boy.

Reared on a coast that was the legendary haunt of pirates, it did not take the boys long to return home, fetch picks and spades and start to dig beneath the tree. Shovelling out the loose earth, they found themselves in a thirteen ft. wide, well-defined circular shaft, its walls of hard clay scored by the marks of picks. At four ft. they unearthed a layer of flagstones. These were not indigenous to the island, but must have been brought from Gold River, about two miles distant.

At the depth of ten ft. they found a platform made of oak logs, extending across the shaft, their ends firmly embedded in its walls. The outside of these logs was so rotten as to suggest they had been embedded there for a great many years. They loosened the logs, hoisted them out and dug downwards. At twenty ft. they encountered another oak platform, and another at thirty ft. The earth between each platform had settled about two ft.

Realizing that the task was too much for them, McGinnis, Smith and Vaughan, leaving sticks to mark the spot, returned to the mainland to seek help in securing the treasure they were convinced lay a few feet further down. It took them nine years to find backers to provide the primitive machinery they required. The island, they were told, was haunted; a woman recalled that her mother, one of the original settlers in the district, had spoken of strange lights and fires at night. A boatload of men had rowed to the island to investigate and had never returned.

Although it was not recorded in print until 1864 (*The Colonist*) the story told by McGinnis, Smith and Vaughan is well authenticated. In 1849 Smith gave the facts to Robert Creelman, who was concerned in the excavations at that date and who lived until 1900. Smith lived on the island until his death in 1857, and his daughter was employed by Judge Mather Des Brisay who in 1870 published his *History of Lunenberg County*, in which he recorded the story of the discovery, and the subsequent excavations.

McGinnis and Smith settled on the island. On 25 June 1795 Smith purchased lot 18, the area surrounding the site of the discovery, and by 1825 he had acquired lots 16, 17, 19 and 20, comprising the twenty-four acres which formed its eastern end. The cove where McGinnis had landed became known as 'Smith's Cove', whether or not in honour of John is uncertain. It was also called 'Smuggler's Cove'.

The island, which was probably already known locally as Oak Island, from its luxuriant growth of red oaks, had been officially named 'No. 28' in 1785, when it was surveyed and divided into plots by William Nelson, of whom nothing is known. A later copy of his survey, made in 1818, survives in the Registry of Deeds at Bridgewater, Nova Scotia. Several plots were allocated in 1785. Lot 18 (that purchased ten years later by John Smith), was taken up by Caspar Wollenhaupt, a merchant of Chester, and another came into the possession of Anthony Vaughan, the father of young Anthony. He sold it in 1790 to Nathaniel Melvin. Vaughan is described by Des Brisay as owning 200 acres of land on the western shore of the bay, on the mainland opposite Oak Island.

None of these landowners seem to have lived on the island or to have cultivated the ground. A road ran down the centre of the main part of the island, from west to east, which divided lots 1-14 on the north side from lots 21-32 on the south side. It may have been constructed at the time of the survey, or it may have existed prior to 1785.

The island was thus well known to the people of Chester. The town had been established in 1759, ten years after the foundation of Halifax, forty miles to the north. Judge Des Brisay records thirty families living in Chester in 1763 and 231 people in 1767.

Following the expulsion of the French 'Acadians', as they were known, at the end of the French and Indian War (1754-63), English, Scottish and German settlers came to Nova Scotia. Their numbers were augmented after 1782 by the influx of American Tories, the 'United Empire Loyalists', who were evacuated from New England at the close of the American Revolution, or the War of American Independence, as the British call it.

The name of the bay is believed to be derived from the French *mahonne*, a low-lying, fast type of sailing ship, originating in the Mediterranean and much used there by pirates. The name is first recorded in the coastal survey made in 1736 by the English navigator, Thomas Durrell. The bay is shown, but incorrectly named 'B. S°. Marguerite', on the French *Carte de L'Acadie* drawn in 1744. The name may have been adopted to record the activities of the French pirates of Le Have, a port forty miles down the coast from Mahone Bay. This small French colony had been established in 1632. Their seamen preyed upon New England shipping about 1700-10. Another map, printed by Thomas Jeffreys (*History of the French Dominions in North and South*

America, London, 1760) and drawn in 1755, depicts Mahone Bay and shows islands at its head.

Mahone Bay had been surveyed three times. Charles Morris, the first Surveyor-General of Nova Scotia, drew four charts in 1762. Oak Island is depicted in three and named in one (B. 5813). Morris called it Smith's Island, the name it might have been given after 1805, when John Smith lived there. There seems little possibility that the name was added later by Morris's sons who, in turn, succeeded him as Surveyor of Lands. Having examined the manuscript chart, the Curator of the British Admiralty Hydrographic Department wrote, 'I cannot imagine that the name Smith's Island was added after it was drawn in 1762'. It was written by the same hand as the other island names. The chart on which the island is named is described as a 'Draught of Mahone Bay'. It is not as clear or as accurate as the other three charts in which the island is unnamed. Possibly, the name 'Smith's' given to the island was a passing whim.

The distinguished British military engineer, John Montrésor, visited the bay in 1768. He drew a chart on which Oak Island is discernible, but is not named. He was followed by the British Admiralty Hydrographer, Joseph Frederick Wallet Des Barres. He drew a detailed chart in 1773. Oak Island is depicted and named, but not as 'Oak' island, the name it acquired locally. (Des Barres's chart later takes on peculiar significance.)

Oak Island lies at latitude 44° 31' N: longitude 64° 18' W: at the head of Mahone Bay, close to the mainland from which it is separated by a narrow, shallow channel. It is completely obscured from the open sea by the Tancook Islands which protect the bay's 240 sq. miles of water from the storms of the Atlantic.

Its geological formation is peculiar. The Canadian Department of Mines geological survey of 1939 shows that the eastern part of the island is formed of limestone, gypsum and sandstone. The western part is composed of quartzite and slate. The island, it is thought, may once have been two islands, a supposition which is supported by the low ground and the swamp which form the narrow neck between the two geologically different parts. The soil at the eastern end is formed of hard blue clay to the depth of approximately 110 ft., and below that of brown marl.

The island's eastern end is not flat, as the numerous air-photographs suggest. From Smith's Cove the ground rises to a small hill, thirty-five ft. above sea level, and then descends gradually towards the south and west. The shaft discovered in 1795 is situated on the south-western slope of this hill, which continues to rise slightly to the north.

In the years ahead this insignificant island was to become the focus of much speculation, interest and excitement.

2 The Sea Surges Up

Work on the site was resumed in 1804, nine years having elapsed since the discovery of the mysterious shaft, the 'Money Pit', as it would soon become known.
The Colonist, 2 January 1864, records:

> The late Simeon Lynds of Onslow, a man well known in many parts of Colchester County, at the time happened to visit Chester on business. As Lynd's father and Vaughan were related, he called and passed an evening with him. In the course of conversation during the night, Lynds was let into the secret of the 'Pit' on Oak Island, and the opinion entertained about it by Vaughan and his companions.
>
> The next day Vaughan crossed over to the place with Simeon Lynds, in a boat, to let him pass his own judgment upon it. The result of Lynds' visit was that he became of Vaughan's way of thinking.
>
> Lynds was then a young man (about thirty years) and his father (Thomas Lynds) was in comfortable circumstances, and he had a good many well-to-do friends. He concluded to go home, form a company among them, to assist the pioneers in the search after the treasure and to complete it.

Lynds formed a syndicate of friends from Halifax, Colchester and Pictou Counties: Colonel Robert Archibald, Captain David Archibald and Sheriff Thomas Harris.

> On their arrival they were joined by the first three treasure seekers, with whom they made arrangements to commence operations.
>
> During the time that had intervened since the leaving of work by the resident diggers, the Pit had caved in and formed the shape of a sugar loaf resting on its apex, and besides, from the action of the rain and weather, a great quantity of mud had settled at the bottom. It gave them some trouble to clear all this out, but when they had done so, they came across the sticks sunk in the mud by the first diggers on the termination of their work. They then felt satisfied that the place had not been interfered with since.
>
> They had not got far into the work that was new to

Vaughan and his former associates, when they struck a second tier of oak logs, corresponding with the first. Ten feet lower down they found a tier of charcoal, and ten feet further a tier of putty.

A small discrepancy appears to arise; in the account of the 1795 operations it is said that the boys encountered three oaken platforms at ten, twenty and thirty ft. levels, which they hoisted out, whereas by *The Colonist*'s account it is implied that they did not reach the second and third tiers until 1804. This is unimportant, but a statement made by Judge Des Brisay, writing in 1870, may be of considerable significance. He says that at the thirty ft. level the 1804 syndicate came upon 'charcoal (and) ten ft. below it, putty'. Another version states that the putty was found at the forty ft. level, spread over a platform of logs and there was so much of it that it served to glaze the windows of more than twenty houses around Mahone Bay. More charcoal and more oak logs were encountered farther down and ten ft. lower, coconut fibre and yet another oaken platform. Local tradition has it that quantities of coconut fibre were removed from the Pit. Hiram Walker, a ship's carpenter of Chester, who was engaged in the operations, told his granddaughter, Mrs Cottnam Smith, that he had seen bushels of coconut fibre brought up from the shaft.

James McNutt, who worked on the island in 1863, and who wrote an account of which only a fragment survives, states that: 'At forty feet a tier of charcoal: at fifty feet a tier of smooth stones from the beach, with figures and letters cut on them; at sixty feet a tier of manilla grass and the rind of the coconut; at seventy feet a tier of putty.'

No authority other than McNutt mentions the tier of smooth beach stones with figures and letters cut upon them. They disappeared without trace, which is not perhaps surprising when we consider the haphazard way in which the early searchers discarded clues which might have helped them to solve the mystery. McNutt recorded an event which is described also by Judge Des Brisay.

At the depth of ninety ft. it would seem the searchers uncovered a flat stone, three ft. long and one ft. wide, on the reverse side of which rude letters and figures had been cut. 'It was,' says McNutt, 'freestone, being different from any on that coast.' The syndicate, recalls Des Brisay, 'were in

17

hopes this inscription would throw some valuable light on their search, but unfortunately they could not decipher it, and it was too badly cut, or did not appear to be in their own vernacular'. 'This remarkable stone,' Des Brisay says, 'was preserved in the family of Mr Smith it may be seen by the curious to the present day (1884).'

Alas, that is no longer true. Like other Money Pit 'exhibits' the inscribed stone had an unfortunate history. John Smith placed it at the back of the fireplace of the house he built on the island close to the Money Pit, where it was seen by many people. Eventually the stone was removed and taken to Halifax where it was exhibited in the windows of A. & H. Creighton Bookbinders, of 64 Upper Walter Street. Creighton was treasurer of the Oak Island Association formed in 1864. He exhibited the stone, in order, no doubt, to sell shares in the company. It was inspected there by James Liechti, Professor of Languages at Dalhousie College, who interpreted the cipher to read: 'TEN FEET BELOW TWO MILLION POUNDS.'

The cipher also appears, with a translation by the Rev. A. T. Kempton, of Cambridge, Massachusetts in a work by Edward Rowe Snow (*Mysteries and Adventures Along the Atlantic Coast*, N.Y. 1948).

The stone was seen at Creighton's by Harry W. Marshall, an employee of the firm, who told Frederick Blair on 27 March 1935:

> I well remember seeing it as a boy and until the business was merged in 1919 in the present firm of Phillips and Marshall.
>
> The stone was about two feet long, fifteen inches wide and ten inches thick, and weighed about 175 pounds. It had two smooth surfaces, with rough sides and traces of cement attached to them. Tradition said that it had been part of two fireplaces. The corners were not squared but somewhat rounded. The block resembled dark Swedish granite, or fine grained porphyry, very hard, and with an olive tinge, and did not resemble any local Nova Scotia stone.
>
> While in Creightons' possession someone had cut his initials 'J.M.' on one corner, but apart from this there was no evidence of any inscription either cut or painted on the stone. It had completely faded out. We used the stone for a beating stone and weight.
>
> When the business was closed, in 1919, Thomas Forhan, since deceased, asked for the stone, the history of which

seems to have been generally known. When we left the premises in 1919 the stone was left behind, but Forhan's business premises and residence two years ago (1933) disclosed no stone.

Captain H. L. Bowdoin, who will be referred to later, saw the stone in 1909. It no longer bore any characters.

Various versions of the inscription have been published. In 1970 I submitted it for decipherment to two British cipher experts, Professor E. R. Vincent, and Mr C. Raymond who translated it to mean 'FORTY FEET BELOW TWO MILLION POUNDS ARE BURIED'. Whether or not the published versions of this inscription are accurate is now beyond corroboration.

The 1804 searchers do not appear to have wasted time trying to decipher the inscription, and they were unaware of the significance of its message, if indeed it had any meaning. Excited by the discovery, which seemed to herald the proximity of the treasure cache, they dug on feverishly. Thrusting a crowbar into the earth, which was becoming so soft and moist that they found themselves raising one cask of water to two of earth, they struck a hard, impenetrable substance at ninety-eight ft. which seemed to stretch across the width of the whole shaft. 'Some', states *The Colonist*'s account, 'supposed it was wood, and others called it a chest.'

It was close to nightfall on a Saturday night. Convinced that they were on the brink of success, the elated treasure seekers climbed from the Pit, so filled with good spirits that they spent the evening discussing who would have the larger share of the treasure. When they returned next morning, or more probably on the Monday, for the Sabbath intervened, they found sixty ft. of water in the Money Pit; it was flooded to within thirty-three ft. of the top. Undaunted, they set to work to bale out the water with buckets. Despite their efforts the water level remained at the same height. Their simple appliances were not sufficient for the emergency. When bailing proved ineffective the syndicate recruited the services of a man named Mosher who rigged up a pump which he lowered to a depth of ninety ft. The pump burst and work was abandoned for the year.

Unfortunately for themselves and for the syndicate that followed them, the 1804 seekers did not stop to consider where the water came from. With the object of draining the Money Pit, they dug another shaft alongside it in the spring of 1805. Reaching the depth of 110 ft. they tunnelled sideways in order to reach the chests they believed lay at ninety-eight ft. They were overwhelmed by a flood of water and they barely escaped with their lives. Overnight the second shaft filled with water, to within thirty-three ft. of the top.

That was the end of the first organized treasure hunt on Oak Island. It had found nothing to confirm or deny the existence of treasure in the Pit other than the 'inscribed stone', the tiers of logs, quantities of charcoal, the putty, the coconut fibre and husk, and the obstruction met with at ninety-eight ft. It was believed that this was one or perhaps two chests, one above the other. No one doubted that the Money Pit was a treasure cache, one probably of immense value, for why otherwise had the shaft been sunk so deep?

3 The Tides of the Ocean

Forty years elapsed before another organized attempt was made to reveal the secrets of the Money Pit.

When a new company was formed in 1845, only Anthony Vaughan remained of the original discoverers to guide its members. Although John Smith lived until September 1857, he does not appear to have been concerned in the new enterprise, other than by expressing his belief in the existence of treasure in the Money Pit. By now McGinnis had disappeared from the scene.

The Truro syndicate – a name derived from the town of its origin – included Dr David Barnes Lynds, John Gammell, Adam A. Tupper and Robert Creelman. Jotham McCully was appointed manager of the operations and James Pitblado was made foreman of the works. Registration of the names of some of the many searchers is important in order to emphasize the continuity of the history of the operations. Several of those concerned talked with their predecessors and successors about their searches.

The active members of the new syndicate landed on the island in 1849. Vaughan located the site of the original shaft which had caved in. So had the adjacent shaft (No. 2) which had been dug nearby to drain the Money Pit, with sufficiently disastrous results, one would have thought, to have discouraged similar enterprises. Re-excavating the original shaft, the new men found, at six ft., part of the pump which had burst in 1805. Twelve days work brought them to a depth of eighty-six ft. The flooding appeared to have subsided. *The Colonist*, 7 January 1864, quotes from an account written by 'a member of the Oak Island Association' of Truro on 22 December 1863:

> They found that it remained exactly as discovered by Simeon Lynds (in 1804) and did not entertain the shadow of a doubt in their own minds, but that the Pit had been sunk by some parties long before Lynds ever saw the place. They worked on successfully for about a fortnight when Saturday night arrived, and all further work was postponed until Monday morning.

Sabbath morning came and no sign of water, more than usual, appearing in the Pit, the men left for church in Chester Village with lighter hearts. At two o'clock they returned from church, and to their great surprise found water standing in the Pit, to the depth of sixty feet, being on a level with that in the Bay.

The next morning they set vigorously to work bailing, and had not long been engaged until the result appeared as unsatisfactory as taking soup with a fork. Notwithstanding the disappointment was great and the difficulty appeared almost insurmountable, they did not feel disposed to drop the work without further efforts.

The water had risen, once again, to within thirty-three ft. of the top of the Pit. The Truro men decided to probe the lower depths by the use of a pod-auger, a primitive type of drill. When it arrived, a platform was erected above the water, and, under the direction of McCully, five holes were bored to a depth of 106 ft. The first hole was made a little to the west of centre of the Pit, the others a little east of one another. In boring the first two holes there was no indication of anything but mud and stones. McCully later made a written statement concerned with the results of the next three holes:

The platform (found in the Pit in 1804) was struck at 98 feet just as the old diggers found it, when sounding with the iron bar. After going through the platform, which was five inches thick, and proved to be spruce, the auger dropped twelve inches and then went through four inches of oak; then it went through twenty-two inches of metal in pieces; but the augur failed to bring up anything in the nature of treasure, except three links resembling the links of an ancient watch chain. It then went through eight inches of oak, which was thought to be the bottom of the first box and the top of the next; then twenty-two inches of metal, the same as before; then four inches of oak and six inches of spruce, then into clay seven feet without striking anything.

In boring the second hole, the platform was struck, as before, at 98 feet; passing through this, the auger fell about eighteen inches and came in contact with (as supposed) the side of a chest. The flat chisel revolving close to the side of the chest gave it a jerky and irregular motion. On withdrawing the auger, several splinters of oak (believed to be from the bilge of a cask) such as might come from the side of an oak stave, a piece of a hoop made of birch and a small

THE MONEY PIT

OAK TREE.
WITH LOPPED BRANCH.

LAYER OF STONES.

10 FEET

20 — OAK PLATFORMS.

30 —

TIDE LEVEL

40 AIRLOCK   OAK PLATFORM SEALED WITH
              PUTTY.

50 —   OAK PLATFORM.

60 AIRLOCK   OAK PLATFORM SEALED WITH
              PUTTY & COCONUT FIBRE.

70 —   OAK PLATFORM.

80 AIRLOCK   OAK PLATFORM SEALED WITH
Stone with cipher. COCONUT FIBRE.

90 AIRLOCK   OAK PLATFORM SEALED WITH
CHESTS?   PUTTY.
100 —   SPRUCE PLATFORM.

110 —   HIGH TUNNEL TO SHORE (SMITH'S COVE)

Puddled
clay
below
110?

150 —   LOW TUNNEL TO SHORE (SMITH'S COVE)

180 FEET   UNDERGROUND STREAM?

quantity of brown fibrous substance, closely resembling the husk of a coconut, were brought up. The difference between the upper and lower platforms was found to be six feet.

These were important discoveries. The borings appeared to confirm the presence, at ninety-eight ft., of a chest, or chests, one above the other, made of oak and resting above a platform built of spruce. Each chest was believed to contain twenty-two-inch lengths of metal, a surmise which seemed to be confirmed by the discovery of 'three links resembling an ancient watch chain'. Another member of the syndicate, Sheriff Thomas Harris, in a letter written many years later, told his grandson of the discovery of 'this piece of gold chain'. But that is the last we hear of it. James McNutt, writing in 1863, refers to the discovery of 'three pieces of copper wire'. He said also that there was brought up a 'sort of grass, the same as found in the Pit at sixty feet, and a substance, white in colour, resembling putty'.

What did these borings really disclose? Did the chests filled with metal and the piece of gold chain exist other than in the fervid imagination of people to whom the wish was father to the thought? We can conclude only that the 1849 borings disclosed objects at the depth of ninety-eight ft. which *may* have been oak chests.

There now occurred an incident which the Truro men, and subsequent treasure seekers, have accepted as irrefutable proof that the Money Pit contained treasure, and still does.

Under the watchful eyes of Dr Lynds, John Gammell and of the other members of the syndicate, James Pitblado, the foreman, was ordered to make a third boring. He was instructed to remove carefully every bit of material brought to the surface by the auger, so that it could be examined under the microscope. Gammell later claimed that he saw Pitblado, when he thought no one was watching him, take something out of the auger, wash it, examine it closely and place it in his pocket. When asked by Gammell to show him what it was, he declined and said that he would show it at the next meeting of the directors. Pitblado failed to attend the meeting, and no one ever learned what it was that he had removed from the auger. Tradition has it that it was a jewel.

Pitblado's further actions appear suspicious. He is said to have left the island and to have sought out Charles Dickson Archibald, the manager of the Arcadian Iron Works, Nova Scotia, who immediately made a determined, though unsuccessful, effort to purchase the eastern part of Oak Island. Pitblado did not return to the island and his fate is obscure.

Encouraged by the supposed results of these borings, or by their own imagination, the Truro men convinced themselves that two oak chests filled with treasure lay immediately below the ninety-eight ft. level. They can hardly be blamed for jumping to conclusions based on such doubtful evidence – the shaft had been sunk for some purpose. What other purpose than for the concealment of vast treasure?

When they returned to the island in the spring of 1850, the Truro men, the true pioneers of the long exploration to reveal the secrets of the Money Pit, sunk a fresh shaft (No. 3) slightly to the west, or north-west, of the original shaft (No. 1) and about ten ft. from it. They dug through hard clay to the depth of 109 ft. without encountering water. Following the example of the 1805 searchers they drove a tunnel towards the Money Pit, but before it was reached, water burst in and forced the workmen to clamber up the shaft to save their lives. Within a few minutes the new shaft was filled with forty-five ft. of water. No amount of bailing or pumping succeeded in reducing the water level in either shaft.

The secret cause of the flooding was discovered by chance. According to a somewhat improbable story, a member of the syndicate fell into the shaft; whether or not this accident actually occurred, the members did learn that the water was sea water, and that it rose and fell with the tide at the rate of one in. to one ft. This was a tremendous clue which the Truro syndicate did not fail to follow up.

The soil of the island was not of a character to invite natural seepage; had the flooding been natural it would have interfered with the original excavations. One other possibility remained: the sea water was carried into the Money Pit by a man-made tunnel which had its inlet somewhere on the shore! This amazing theory was quickly confirmed. A search on the beach at Smith's Cove, 500 ft. from the Money Pit, provided the answer. As the tide ebbed, the sand and shingle 'gulched water like a sponge being squeezed'. Rivulets of water gushed down the beach as if it came from many bubbling springs. A number of large boulders had been removed from the central part of the beach and had been piled at its sides. A few hours of shovelling provided an amazing discovery.

On removing the sand and gravel to a depth of three ft., the workmen came upon a layer, about two in. deep, of brown, fibrous plant, the same as had been discovered in the Money Pit. Beneath it they found a layer of four to five in. of eel-grass, or kelp, tons of which were removed and piled on the beach like hay-cocks. Still farther down they encountered a mass of flat stones, laid criss-cross and free from sand and gravel.

This giant, man-made 'sponge' extended along the beach, between high and low water marks, for 145 ft. The inference was clear. The original depositors, to protect their treasure cache, had harnessed the tides of the ocean. The sea water was carried to the Money Pit by a subterranean tunnel, 500 ft. from Smith's Cove. Each high tide replenished the water in the tunnel.

Further excavation revealed the extent, and the ingenuity, of the drains by which the tunnel was supplied. Five well-built box-drains, formed of flat stones set eight in. apart at a depth of five ft., and covered over with larger stones, formed a fan-like drain which converged to a funnel-shaped sump hole set just above high water mark. *The Colonist* of 2 January 1864 records this discovery:

> In investigating the drains they found that they connected with one of large dimensions, the stones forming which had been prepared with a hammer, and were mechanically laid in such a way that the drain could not collapse. There were a number of tiers of stones strengthening the higher part of the drain, on the top of which was also found a coating of the same sort of grass as that already noticed. Over it came a layer of blue sand, such as before had not been seen on the island, and over the sand was spread the gravel indigenous to the coast.
>
> Having laid bare the large drain for a short distance into the bank, they found it had been so well made and protected that no earth had sifted through the arch to obstruct water passing through it.
>
> They then attempted to follow the inward direction of the drain in search of a perpendicular shaft, but on account of the surrounding soil being so soft, and so much saturated with water, it was given up as impracticable.

Captain Anthony Vaughan, the son of the discoverer (who died in New York in 1948 at the age of a hundred), informed an investigator in 1938 that he remembered as a boy aged ten being present when the five drains were uncovered at Smith's Cove.

Of all the strange facts about Oak Island which have been disclosed, none has caught the public imagination more than the discovery of the water catchment and the flood tunnel by which the mystery men of long ago sought to protect their concealment – if, in fact, that was their purpose. They did far more than dig a deep shaft, in itself a herculean task. They ran from it a subterranean tunnel to the beach where they constructed a 'catchment' 145 ft. in length. This flood tunnel, it was subsequently revealed, is three and a half ft. high, two and a half ft. wide, and climbs from the Pit to the sump hole by the beach, it was estimated by those who inspected it, at a gradient of twenty-two and a half degrees. Full realization of the magnitude of this feat of engineering achieved by the men of Oak Island needs to await description of further events. However even at this stage, we begin to marvel.

The treasure seekers of 1850 now had some idea of what they were up against but they rose to the new challenge. They went to the enormous labour and cost of constructing, below high water mark, a coffer dam 150 ft. long and high enough to hold back the tides, intending to enclose the centre of Smith's Cove, thus achieving the destruction of the source of the water supply. Before the work could be completed, the dam was destroyed by an unusually high tide. Its semicircular outline can still be discerned in aerial photographs.

The Truro searchers were the first to conceive the possibility that somewhere below ground there exists a set of water gates by which it was once possible to cut off the flow of water to the Pit, an improbable feature which has neither been proved nor disproved by the operations on the island.

Unable to destroy the source of water supply to the Pit, the workmen attempted to find the tunnel's course. They sank fresh shafts and tunnelled sideways. The recorded statements about these, and later shafts and tunnels, are highly confusing; several cannot have been sunk or driven at the places indicated. The sites of others are improbable. (The likely location of these shafts and tunnels is examined in

27

Appendix B.) The Truro men are said to have started work at a spot 140 ft. to the east of the Pit in an attempt to locate the flood tunnel. They sank their shaft (No. 4) to the depth of seventy-five feet without encountering it. Realizing that they had missed the tunnel, they re-started twelve ft. to the south of shaft No. 5. At the depth of thirty-five ft. they came across a large boulder. An attempt to try to pry it out resulted in a rush of water and within a few minutes the new shaft was filled to tide level. The water proved to be salt. Its presence in the shaft was taken to prove that the flood tunnel had been reached. Stakes and heavy timbers were driven down but they failed to halt the rush of water into the Money Pit.

Having as they thought, located the flood tunnel, the syndicate members sank another shaft (No. 6) on the south side and within fifty ft. of the Money Pit. Reaching a depth of 118 ft. they drove a tunnel, three ft. by four ft., towards the original shaft. The workmen knocked off for dinner. Most of the men were absent when disaster struck.

The Pit caved in and collapsed into the tunnel which had been driven at 118 ft. Several workmen were dragged to safety. The searchers believed that, in the cataclysm, their so-called 'treasure chests' dropped into the void below, where they lodged at 150 ft. below the surface.

The Truro company's capital was by now exhausted. An appeal for further funds brought no response. The collapse of the Pit ended the syndicate's early operations on the island. It had achieved something; the secret of the flooding had been disclosed.

4 Bailing out the Ocean

John Smith died in 1857. His property was acquired by Anthony Graves who built a house and a barn and cultivated land at the 'neck' of the island, between the swamp and the landing place on the north shore. It became known as Jodrey's Cove. During his thirty years' residence on the island, Graves is reputed to have purchased supplies around Mahone Bay using Spanish coins and, in 1930, when his son-in-law pulled down his old house, two Spanish coins dated 1785 were found at the side of the old road. An excavation nearby suggested that Graves had been searching for treasure. Discovery of ancient coins is not an unusual occurrence around Mahone Bay, which was once the haunt of pirates. I was told, for example, about two spinsters whose father left them a box packed with gold coins, great wealth which the ladies continued to hoard.

Yet a coin dated 1785 is unlikely to have formed part of a pirate's cache. Pirates had long disappeared from the Atlantic. It is equally difficult to link a coin of that date with the Money Pit, discovered in 1795 on an island which had been surveyed and its land apportioned ten years earlier.

Graves, who died in 1887, was assisted in his farming and succeeded by his two daughters, Sophia who married Henry Sellers, and Rachel who married Abraham Ernest, both local men. In 1887 Mrs Sellers' oxen fell into a 'well-like' hole.

Meanwhile curious visitors continued to arrive on the island. In 1857 the geologist, Henry S. Poole, having visited the island and inspected the Pit, made the following report to the Government of Nova Scotia:

> I crossed to Oak Island and observed slate all the way along the main shore but I could not see any rock *in situ* on the Island. I went to the spot where people had been engaged for so many years searching for the supposed hidden treasure of Captain Kidd. I found the original shaft had caved in, and two others had been sunk alongside. One was open and said to be 120 feet deep, and in all that depth no rock had been struck. The excavated matter alongside was composed

of sand and boulder rocks and though the pit was some two hundred yards from the shore, the water in the shaft (which I measured to be within thirty-three feet of the top) rose and fell with the tide, showing a free communication between the sea and the shaft.

The Truro men made a fresh attempt to recover the treasure in 1859, according to A. I. Spedon who visited the island in 1862 (*Rambles Among The Blue Noses*, 1863):

Up to the present moment the work has been resumed and relinquished a dozen times. Companies have been formed again and again, numerous experiments tried, and no less than fifteen different pits have been dug, at a cost of many thousands of dollars; and yet the *mysterious* box appears not to have been found. The most determined and untiring adventures of the 'treasure diggers' are those comprising the company at Truro, whose operations alone, during the last ten years, have incurred an expense of no less than twenty thousand dollars.   ...

During my stay at Halifax, and afterwards, I repeatedly heard of the 'mysterious treasure', but considered the whole affair as only a fictitious tale, or a chimerical infatuation, until I had met with Mr McCully, Secretary-Treasurer of the company, who narrated the whole events and persuaded me at length to visit the island.

The operations of this company have been immense. The great obstruction and difficulty has been the inexhaustible quantity of water in the Pit. It appears to come from the sea, but no experiment has yet been enabled to remove it, or stem the current. Deep pits have again and again been dug near to the old one, and connected by subterraneous channels, formed for the purpose of diverting the current. One pit was even sunk to the depth of ninety feet.

During the summer of 1859, the company had no less than thirty horses employed at the pumps, but all efforts have proved abortive.

In the fall of 1861, at great expense, pumps were erected to be driven by steam power, but scarcely had the works been commenced when the boiler burst, causing operations to be suspended until another season.

One man died from scalding in this accident and several others were injured. E. H. Owen of Lunenburg, describing how the water from the Money Pit was pumped out through a large barrel-shaped tube and conveyed to the shore along a long wooden trough, comments:

I visited the island in September last (1862) at which time the engine was working well; but strange to say, the water continued to retain its level without apparently any diminution. Discouraged and disappointed, the company at length yielded to prudence and common sense and relinquished their claim for ever, but not until necessity had compelled them to comply therewith.

Every indication and circumstances relative to the reality of such deposits appear to render it very probable that there is more fact than fiction connected therewith. Oaken boxes have been bored through apparently filled with gold. West Indian grass and other foreign substances, together with many other indications, have been found from time to time in the Pit.

A. I. Spedon had his own theories:

It appears that in digging the Pit in which he (Captain Kidd) deposited his gold, he connected with it a subterraneous passage, leading towards the shore, by which means he might be enabled to recover his gold, without having to excavate the Pit which he had filled up with such substance as would render it almost impenetrable to the enemy, if discovered.

Further from the continued presence of water, as well as from the existence of oak trees, beyond the extremities of the island, growing as it were out of the sea, it appears that the watermark of a hundred years ago (1760) has sunk far below the present one (1860); hence may arise the current of water along the subterraneous channel to the Pit, or perhaps it may also arise from some other source in connection with the sea.

[Captain Kidd was an early favourite for the role of the depositor of the treasure.]

Several searchers shared Spedon's opinion that the tunnel from the shore provided a passage into the Money Pit by which entry could be made into the treasure chamber, believed to exist ninety-eight ft. down. Somewhere along the tunnel a gate had been provided by which the rush of water could be cut off. This seems improbable, for no system of lock gates, even if practicable to construct, could survive the continual flow of sea-water and remain serviceable. Spedon may have been correct in thinking that the erosion of the shore, and the consequent rise of sea level at Smith's Cove, may have increased the flow of sea-water from the Cove into the tunnel.

It is thought that heavy erosion has eaten away the island's shore at a rate of two ft. every hundred years. The Marine Sciences Branch of the Canadian Department of Mines and Technical Surveys informed me on 11 March 1965, 'the water level around Oak Island has risen 0.5 of a foot during the last forty years'. The general rise along the Atlantic coast has not been less than one inch.

Another Truro syndicate was formed in 1860. This 'Oak Island Association', as it was called, included Adam A. Tupper, Jotham B. McCully and James McNutt of the original company, and the new adventurer, Jefferson W. McDonald. McNutt kept a record of the syndicate's operations, which came into the possession of Frederick Blair. An agreement was reached with Anthony Graves, the current owner of the property, who was guaranteed one-third of the value of any treasure recovered, and the operations recommenced.

The Truro syndicate attempted to drain the Money Pit and the adjacent shafts. They installed a powerful pump and set a force of sixty-three men to work. Assisted by thirty-three horses, they filled and emptied several seventy-gallon casks but fifty hours of continuous pumping and bailing succeeded only in forcing the water down to the eighty-two ft. level. Several workmen descended into the adjacent shaft and attempted to reach the Pit through the tunnel the company had driven previously but rushes of water and soft clay forced them back. The debris included a piece of juniper tree, its bark intact, which had been cut at each end with an edged tool. Other objects included a piece of oak three ft. long and six in. in diameter; a slab of spruce which contained a bore hole – perhaps part of the obstruction bored through in 1849; and quantities of fibrous material which was identified as coconut fibre.

The cribbing in the Money Pit had collapsed and it could no longer be entered with safety. The water in shaft No. 5, which had been sunk in 1850, rose and fell with the tide, though from where it received sea-water at a thirty-five ft. level at that spot defies comprehension.

Following the abortive attempt to pump and bail out the Money Pit, the new Truro syndicate adopted the tactics of their predecessors: they attempted to trace and intercept the water tunnel from Smith's Cove. To achieve this end they sank a new shaft (No. 7) 107 ft. deep, close to the

Money Pit on its western side. Their excavations disclosed tools abandoned by both the Onslow Company of 1804 and the Truro Company of 1850, indicating that the new shaft was adjacent to or within shaft No. 3. They found no evidence of the water tunnel; it would have been surprising if they had, for they were working on the wrong side of the Money Pit. When the new shaft filled with water, they sank yet another shaft (No. 8), also on the west side of the Money Pit close to No. 6, that sunk in 1850.

They returned to Smith's Cove where they attempted to block the drains leading from the beach. They packed them with clay but it was washed away by the incoming tide. They then returned to the Money Pit and sunk another shaft (No. 9) a hundred ft. to its south-east and twenty ft. south of the supposed line of the flood tunnel. Digging to the depth of 120 ft., they drove two tunnels, one northwards and the other southwards, without locating the flood tunnel. Why they ran one in the opposite direction from the supposed line of the flood tunnel is hard to understand. A third tunnel driven towards the shore achieved no better success. A fourth tunnel directed to the north-west entered the side of the Money Pit at a point 108 ft. down.

According to the records, the operators set the pump to work and succeeded in pumping the Money Pit dry to the depth of 180 ft. This figure seems to be inaccurate. J. B. Leedham, who was in charge of the operations, stated (*Colchester Sun*, 21 August 1894) that he descended to 108 ft., probably the depth to which the level of water had been lowered.

In his descent, Leedham noticed that on one side of the Pit, the walls and floor were hard, but so soft elsewhere that a crowbar could be sunk. The workmen ran another tunnel near the Pit at the 108 ft. level, locating on the way shaft No. 2, which had been sunk by the original syndicate in 1804.

These operations convinced the searchers that the supposed treasure chests, which had formerly rested on a platform about a hundred ft. down, had fallen only ten ft. during the collapse and had not, as had been previously thought, fallen to 150 ft. The Truro men seemed to have reached the conclusion on very slender evidence.

Once again the company ran out of funds. Unable to raise further capital it ceased to operate in 1865. Nevertheless, the story is still told round Mahone Bay that these Truro men in fact found the treasure. At nightfall, after they had pumped the Money Pit dry, the workmen left the island; when they returned next morning, the members of the syndicate had gone, taking all their equipment in their ship. The workmen had no complaints for they had been paid up to date, but they believed that during the night their employers found the treasure and slipped away. The story is improbable. Had they won the treasure, surely one member of the syndicate at least, would have boasted that he and his friends had succeeded where so many had failed? Nor does it appear that any of those men suddenly became wealthy. (This may not be a very good criterion for, as I was informed in Nova Scotia, 'the really rich are the ones you would least expect'.)

In March 1866, the directors of the Truro Company assigned their rights to the 'Oak Island Eldorado Company'. It became known as the 'Halifax Company' after its place of origin.

5 A Maze of Shafts; a Labyrinth of Tunnels

All the long succession of treasure hunters who attempted to wrest the supposed treasure from the embrace of the watery monster set to guard the island's secrets believed that they would succeed. Undeterred by the failure of others, they blundered into the same morass, and for the same reason: they dug first and thought afterwards, if they thought at all. Yet avarice and greed were not primary motives; countless men have pitted their wits against the Money Pit because 'it is there'. It is a magnetic challenge, drawing adventurers and investigators from all over the world.

The full secrets of the Money Pit were still unknown. Even now, over a hundred years later, they have not been completely disclosed. If, as some sceptics claim, the Money Pit is a monument to human folly, it constitutes an even greater memorial to the genius of its designer, the man whom six generations of 'moderns' have failed to outwit.

The operations of the Halifax Company are cloaked in mystery. Work has been attributed to them which they may not have done, for it is inconceivable that they could have constructed the labyrinth of tunnels with which they are credited. If the tunnels found in the 1938-43 period were *not* dug by the Halifax Company, however, there seems only one other possible explanation – they were part of the original work. The company's operations were recorded by James McNutt and his diary notes nothing to confirm the hasty conclusions that have been drawn about these tunnels.

The company raised $4,000, which, according to the Prospectus, its members intended to spend in building 'a substantial wood and clay dam seaward to extend out and beyond the rock work, so as to encompass the whole within the dam, to pump out all the water within the area, and so block up the inlet from the sea'. 'There cannot be any doubt,' stated the Prospectus, 'but that this mode of operation must succeed and will lead to the development of the treasure so long sought for.'

The company's plan ended in failure. The workmen succeeded in emptying the enclosed area but the dam was destroyed by the tides. Its members repeated the errors of their predecessors. They attempted to re-excavate the Money Pit without first cutting off the water supply. They cleared it out to 108 ft. aided by pumps. Then a workman named Robinson felt the earth give way beneath his feet and lost his pick into the cavity below. The pumps could not cope with the quickly rising water and he was driven from the Pit.

Then the company tried boring. Building a platform at the ninety ft. level and employing a drill set in a three in. pipe, they bored from 26 November 1866 to 7 January 1867. McNutt made a day-by-day record of these operations.

Working at the north-eastern corner of the Money Pit it was recorded that the drill encountered spruce wood at 106 ft., and then coarse gravel and soft clay for a further sixteen ft. Below that depth it penetrated more soft clay and mud. At 125 ft. water flowed up the pipes, carrying chips of wood, charcoal and fibre. At 134 ft. the drill brought up bits of oak and more fibre. It appeared to run alongside what was thought to be a plank. The flow of water stopped and re-started. Thrust down to 158 ft. the drill disclosed a reddish brown material. Two further borings made on the east side of the Pit to depths of 163 ft. and 160 ft. brought no significant results.

These negative findings prompted the members of the syndicate to proceed on different lines. With the object of intercepting the flood tunnel from Smith's Cove, they sank a new shaft (No. 10) about 175 ft. southwards of the supposed line of the tunnel, and 110 ft. deep and drove various lateral tunnels from it. The site of shaft No. 10 is uncertain, it seems to have been positioned to the south-east of the Money Pit and almost a hundred ft. distant.

S. C. Fraser, the company's foreman, implies that the flood tunnel was breached:

The Halifax Company's work was at a base of 110 feet, except two circling tunnels which were on a higher level. As we entered the old place of the treasure (by a tunnel) we cut off the mouth of the 'pirate tunnel'. As we opened it, the water hurled around rocks about twice the size of a man's head, with many smaller, and drove the men back for protection. We could not go into the shaft again for about nine hours. Then the pumps conquered and we went down and cleared it out. The water tunnel was found near the top of our tunnel. I brought Mr Hill, the engineer, down and he put his arm into the hole of the tunnel, up to his shoulder. Nothing could have been more particular than our search in the old place of the old treasure. There was no mistake about our search of the old place.

Fraser was more enlightening in the letter he wrote on 19 June 1895 to A. S. Lowden; 'It [the tunnel] was made of round stones, such as are found abundantly on the beach and fields around the island. Where we found it was the mouth of it, where it empties on to the treasure before it, the treasure went down. We made no effort to stop the flow of water from the drain, first we were at the wrong end, and, again, with the pumps going we could not.'

Thus, according to Fraser, the Halifax men found the mouth of the flood tunnel where it reached the Money Pit at 110 ft. depth.

The Halifax syndicate are credited with the maze of tunnels which have been traced beneath the eastern slopes of the little hill, near the shore at Smith's Cove and extending even beneath the beach. It is unlikely that the company could have executed work of such magnitude in the short time its members were on the island. Significantly, Fraser does not mention such work being done.

Nevertheless the Halifax Company had succeeded in establishing the point at which the flood tunnel entered the Money Pit. They found the tunnel to be two and a half ft. wide and four ft. high, with a down grade of twenty-two and a half degrees. It gushed water and appeared to be filled with rocks and was thought too small to have been intended as an entrance to the treasure chamber. It was still believed that a water gate had been provided with which to halt the flooding which rendered the excavation of the Money Pit unavailing. Why, it was asked, had 'they', the unknown men of the past, gone to such extraordinary ingenuity and labour to construct an impregnable concealment? Surely, a simple hole in the ground would have been enough to guard even the greatest treasure? The answer appeared absurdly simple. The treasure was so immense that it required the tides of the ocean to guard it!

The Halifax Company ended its operations in 1867. One of its members, Isaac Blair, before his death in 1938, told his nephew, Frederick Blair, 'I saw enough to convince me that there was treasure buried there and enough to convince me that they will never get it.'

6 The Guessing Game

Although no major operations were undertaken between 1867 and 1894 two incidents occurred which require later discussion, and several minor discoveries were made.

A whistle, made of bone or ivory, was found on the shore of Smith's Cove in 1885. This was wrongly described as a 'bosun's whistle', which, according to the National Maritime Museum, Greenwich, England, 'were always made of silver or plated'. Another whistle, about three in. long, was found in 1901. It was also made of bone or ivory and was shaped like a violin. Another discovery, prior to 1895, was a copper coin weighing an ounce and a half, dated in one version of the story, 1317, and in a more probable account, 1713. The coin is reputed to have borne 'various strange devices'.

None of these finds provided any clue to the identification of the mystery men who had dug the Money Pit, the puzzle which had intrigued searchers from the time of the Pit's discovery. The fibrous material, quantities of which had been found in the original shaft and in the catchment at Smith's Cove, was believed to provide such a clue. It was thought to be coconut fibre.

In 1916 samples were submitted to the Smithsonian Institute of Washington, DC, which reported: 'The specimen of fibre submitted is undoubtedly from the fibrous husks surrounding a coconut. This fibre is especially resistant to the effects of sea water and under the conditions under which it was found may have been there for several hundred years.'

The Curator of the Institute, Dr Frederick L. Newton, made a similar report in 1930.

The Bureau of Plant Industries, Washington, DC, to which a sample was sent in 1937, failed to identify it, other than by stating that 'unquestionably it is the fibro-vascular tissue of some plant'. In the same year the Botanical Museum of Harvard University, to which another sample had been sent, gave its opinion that 'it is readily distinguishable as manilla hemp'. The external appearances were misleading, the report stated, but 'typical manilla hemp fibres are to be noted in a microscopic examination of the macerated material'.

Whether or not this fibre came from the husks of coconuts, it does seem to have been a tropical material. This suggests that the men who brought it to Oak Island came from, or had visited, the West or possibly the East Indies, where the coconut flourishes. The place of its origin is unknown. It certainly grew in the West Indies in 1725. Sir Hans Sloane states in his book (*Natural History of Jamaica*, Vol. II, 1725) that it formed the staple diet of the natives.

The fibre's usual identification as ship's 'dunnage' seems to be incorrect. Falconer's *Marine Dictionary*, 1780 (reprinted, David and Charles, 1970), defines dunnage as: 'Fardage (FR.) a quantity of faggots, boughs of trees or other loose wood, laid on the bottom of a ship, either to raise the heavy goods which might make her too stiff, or to keep the cargo sufficiently above the bottom, that it may sustain no damage from the water, if the ship should prove leaky.'

Lacking any substantial evidence, the early searchers tried to guess who had dug the Money Pit and constructed its impregnable defences. Pirates were an obvious choice and one pirate in particular seemed to provide the perfect answer.

In popular imagination, Captain William Kidd had become the arch-pirate, the legendary depositor of immense treasure. His hoard had been sought all over the world. His own last words proved its existence. On the night before his execution at Wapping, London, on 23 May 1701, Kidd had written to the Speaker of the House of Commons:

> In my proceedings in the Indies, I have lodged goods and Treasure to the Value of one hundred thousand pounds, which I desiere the Government may have the benefit of, in order thereto I shall desiere no manner of liberty but to be kept prisoner on board such shipp as may be appointed for that purpose and only give the necessary directions and in case I faile therein I shall desiere no favour but to be forthwith Executed according to my sentence.

Kidd was probably bluffing, hoping to gain a stay of execution.

The first reliable reference to Kidd occurs in 1689 when he married, in New York, the wealthy widow Sarah Oort, who had outlived two rich husbands. Following his marriage,

Kidd became a respected and proverbially wealthy merchant, being described as 'William Kidd, Gentleman', a high tribute to his standing in the community. He commanded a privateer in the West Indies in 1690. While he was ashore on the island of Marie Galante, his crew, some of whom were former pirates, seized his ship and sailed her to Nova Scotia. Kidd returned to New York where he was given command of another privateer. It is claimed that he took part in the 1694 expedition led by Sir William Phipps, the Royal Governor of Massachusetts Bay, against the French in 'Acadia', as Nova Scotia was then named. This theory is based on no stronger evidence than that Phipps's fleet included a vessel named the *Adventure*, a similar name to the vessel Kidd commanded in the following year.

Whether or not Kidd took part in Phipps's expedition, his reputation as a brave and experienced seaman earned him in 1695 a privateering commission, registered under the Great Seal of England, to clear the pirates from the Indian Ocean. His ship was named *Adventure Galley*. In the course of his voyage, Kidd turned pirate, technically at least, for he failed to bring his prizes into port as the law required. One prize, the *Quedah Merchant*, yielded a rich haul. He sailed her to the West Indies where her fate is obscure. Following Kidd's arrest at Boston, his loot (valued at £14,000) was unearthed on Gardiners Island, New York, and the £6,000 in his possession was seized by the Crown. He was sent to England for trial rightly or wrongly, convicted of piracy and murder.

One fact is clear. Kidd had no opportunity to visit Nova Scotia between his return from the Indian Ocean in April 1699 and his transportation to England and certainly not to spend months digging and tunnelling on Oak Island. If he ever concealed a great treasure it must have been early in his career. Some authors claim that in about 1669 Kidd traded with the pirates in the West Indies. The dramatic discovery of four charts in the 1930s gives some substance to this belief.

Hubert Palmer, a retired lawyer, lived at Eastbourne, Sussex. He and his brother Guy were indefatigable collectors of pirate relics. In the words of a man who knew them well, 'they were shrewd and discriminating collectors, quick to detect anything spurious and who accepted nothing into their collection until it passed the most rigorous and intensive tests as to its genuineness'.

In 1929 Palmer purchased a heavy seventeenth-century oak bureau from a London collector. It bore a brass plate inscribed CAPTAIN WILLIAM KIDD, ADVENTURE GALLEY, 1669. That was the name of the vessel he commanded in 1695.

Aware that furniture of that period often contained secret compartments, Palmer examined the bureau. He found three hiding places that were unknown to the previous owner, all empty. During a further search, he leaned too heavily on the open lid and one of its runners broke off. He saw on it the barely discernible words, CAPTAIN KIDD, HIS CHEST and found within the runner a narrow brass tube with a tightly rolled piece of yellowish parchment around it. It was a chart of an island, bearing the words, CHINA SEA, and the initials W.K. and the date 1669. There was no clue to the island's location. This tantalizing discovery intensified Palmer's search for further Kidd relics.

In 1931 he purchased an old sea chest from Miss Pamela Hardy, who assured Palmer that it had descended in her family from her ancestor, the famous Captain Thomas Masterman Hardy, of HMS *Victory*, Nelson's Captain at Trafalgar. He had bought it from the grandson of Ned Ward, Kidd's bo'sun, to whom the condemned man had given it the night before his execution, with the threat that if he ever broke it open Kidd's ghost would haunt him. Carved upon the chest's lid was a representation of the skull and crossbones, the date 1669, and the words CAPTAIN KIDD. HIS CHEST. Did the chest, like the bureau, contain a secret compartment?

Palmer noticed that the nails at the bottom of the chest were really screws. Their removal disclosed a false bottom in which he found an old book dated 1662. Beneath it lay a piece of ancient parchment bearing a map of the same unidentified island.

Convinced that other charts existed, Palmer redoubled his enquiries for Kidd relics. In 1932 he was approached by a retired ship's captain named Daniel Morgan, who offered him another chest. It had been taken, he stated, from Newgate Gaol by his ancestor who had been a gaoler there. It bore a brass plate inscribed with the monogram 'K' and the skull and crossbones. Behind the small mirror at the back, Palmer found yet another parchment. The same island had been drawn, now embellished with hills, woods, valleys, coral reefs, lagoon, compass bearings, latitude and longitude, and notes relating to bearings and directions. Across the chart ran a zig-zag line of crosses and other marks drawn in red ink.

Palmer found another relic in 1934, this time in the Channel Island of Jersey. It bore the words WILLIAM AND SARAH KIDD, THEIR BOX, and it too contained a secret compartment which divulged a chart of the same island, larger and more detailed than the previous charts with an anchorage and three wrecks off-shore marked. It provided a totally different set of directions, apparently for locating caches, possibly indicated by three tiny circles.

All four charts were sold privately in 1950 after Palmer's death by Mrs Elizabeth Dick, his housekeeper. They were purchased by an Englishman who went to live in Canada, where I contacted him. 'The charts,' he told me, 'are fading badly.'

While these charts were still in Mrs Dick's possession they were examined by the late R. A. Skelton, then Superintendent of the Map Room at the British Museum, an acknowledged authority on ancient cartography. He considered that they were genuine seventeenth-century charts, conforming in type, ink, parchment and handwriting to charts of that period and confirmed his opinion in 1965 on my enquiry. The charts were photographed at the British Museum by infra-red process in an endeavour to clarify the faded sections but several uncertainties remain.

The charts present one apparent anomaly: it would have been unusual for charts of that period to record longitude. Navigators did not begin to reckon their longitude East or West of Greenwich until 1675 when the Royal Observatory was built. Earlier navigators reckoned their longitude East of the island of Ferro, the most westerly point of the Azores: there was no westerly longitude. Thus, on a Ferro chart the longitude of Oak Island would have been shown as 315° 43′. A missing figure in the longitude given on the Kidd-Palmer chart makes the stated value impossible to determine.

It is difficult to question the authenticity of these charts. The articles in which they were found were apparently genuine Kidd relics. Palmer did not possess the requisite skills to fake them, nor, it seems, could they have been forged before they came into his possession. If they are fakes, it means that someone a very long time ago, planted them in four separate articles of furniture where they might never have been found. But their discovery seems to have been most fortuitous.

The meagre facts of Kidd's known career hardly suggest that he could have amassed great wealth in 1669 when he must have been a young man if, as is assumed, he was born about 1645. It is possible that he stole or copied the charts, or drew them to conform to information he had gleaned.

The discovery of these charts has been described by Anthony Howlett ('The Mystery of Captain Kidd's Treasure', *Wide World Magazine*, October 1958). Mrs Dick had given him 'full access' to the charts.

Howlett, a lawyer, who served with the Royal Navy during the Second World War, believes that he has, with the aid of an ex-naval captain who knows the China Sea, identified Kidd's island, by rationalization of the latitude and longitude given on the charts and with the help of his friend's knowledge of a particular island on which he had once landed. They believe that their identification is confirmed by an Admiralty chart and mention of the island in 1599. Naturally, Mr Howlett is reticent about the island's location.

He was astonished when I said that the island depicted on the charts could be Oak Island, Nova Scotia – but there are remarkable similarities. The label CHINA SEA, an incorrect latitude and longitude, and semi-reversed compass bearings, could have been placed on the charts to make the island's correct identification more difficult. Nova Scotia, incidentally, lies exactly half way round the world, in the Northern Hemisphere, from the China Sea. Or, as a correspondent has remarked, the word 'china' may be derived from the French word 'la Chêne', for oak. In this interpretation 'China Sea' would represent the 'sea', the 200 yards of water, between Oak Island and the mainland.

Comparison of the charted island with modern photographs shows remarkable similarities. One end of 'Kidd's' island looks like the eastern end of Oak Island, and although the rest of the island is dissimilar that may not be a serious objection. Even skilled eighteenth-century surveyors were unable to depict the island's shape with the accuracy of a modern aerial photograph. Since their day erosion has further changed the shore-line. To make a fairer test, I compared one 'Kidd' chart with Des Barres' survey of 1774: I had his *Gloucefter Ifle* (as he named Oak Island) enlarged. Here the similarities are even more marked: he shows a group of rocks where the lagoon once existed, as does the Kidd Chart; he depicts a deep indentation on the northern shore where the chart names 'SMUGGLERS COVE'; Kidd's 'ANCHORAGE', which is indicated by a black mark, approximate to the position of Smith's Cove, and the boulder in which a ring-bolt was found affixed in 1795.

The chart also depicts a triangle in reverse on the opposite shore, its apex pointing out to sea, at approximately the spot where a stone triangle has been found on Oak Island. One part of the legend reads 'Centre of tri . . .' Three 'WRECKS' are marked off that shore, at about the places where old Mahone Bay fishermen have located the skeletons of three ancient vessels. The three tiny circles on the chart approximates to the position of the Money Pit.

The other detailed map, that was found in Daniel Morgan's chest, shows the lagoon, a range of dots running up the island, and a curious little half-circle against the shore, near the anchorage. Could this have depicted the water-catchment?

One statement on the first chart seemed capable of verification. On the shore, some way north of the anchorage, occur the words 20 TURTLES. I wondered if turtles frequented the cold waters of Mahone Bay. (Four varieties of turtle frequent the China Sea.)

An article published in *The Canadian Field Naturalist* (Vol. 79, No. 2, pp. 120-8, April-June 1965) 'Reports of Marine Turtles from New England and Eastern Canada', written by J. Sherman Bleakney, Biology Department, Acadia University, Wolfville, Nova Scotia, provided the information I wanted. There have been many sightings and several captures of turtles, both the hard-shell and the leatherback variety, on the Atlantic coast of Nova Scotia. This had been confirmed by the Smithsonian Institution of Washington, DC, who say: 'There are records of this turtle having been found on the Nova Scotian coast regularly over the past several hundred years.' These turtles swim northwards in July, August and September, in pursuit of the jellyfish upon which they feed.

My other query arose from the use of the term 'SMUGGLERS COVE'. Surely there were no 'smugglers' before the early years of the eighteenth century? They were brought into being by the heavy excise duties imposed in England to pay for Marlborough's wars. A check with the British Customs and Excise enlightened me. In the seventeenth century the expression 'smuggling' would probably have implied the illegal import and export of goods to and from the American colonies, which was prohibited by the British Navigation Acts of 1647, 1651, 1660 and 1663. It was thus a feasible name for a cove on the American coast at that time, but unlikely to be applied to an island in the China Sea.

The directions given on the chart are meaningless. The set displayed on Chart 1 are as follows:

515 S.E. AND BY 50 N.
36 N. E.   36 N. E. ROCKS.
3 FEET BY 3 FEET BY FOUR.

I reconstructed those on Chart II thus:

360 yards V.R. ('v meaning the triangle 'Reversed'?) NORTH
3 stumps 55 FEET
. . . centre of tri(angle) Rocks
20 feet E
Skele(ton) (Drop through?) L(eft) eb(e).

The similarity between the last line and the theme of Edgar Allan Poe's famous story, *The Gold Bug*, is remarkable. He describes how a treasure cache, which he attributed to Kidd, is found by dropping a line through the eye hole of a skull suspended in a tree. Poe wrote the story in 1828 when he was living in South Carolina, where he is reputed to have collected local traditions.

I cannot explain the apparent similarities between Oak Island and the island depicted in the 'Kidd-Palmer' charts, as they are known. A date around 1669 is far too early for the construction of the Money Pit. The tree that so conveniently provided a hoist could have then been no more than a sapling. The charts constitute a mystery within the mystery.

Despite this obvious objection, Kidd has remained first choice as the skilled engineer who set out to baffle and frustrate those who might stumble upon his shaft. One operator facetiously named his lodgement on the island 'CAMP KIDD'.

A similar objection applies to another popular identification. Some investigators believe that the famous 'Buccaneers' established the Money Pit as a communal bank; each captain tunnelling sideways from the depths to create a private cache. Between 1630 and 1670 these 'Brethren of the Coast', as they styled themselves, acted as England's unofficial navy in the Caribbean, looting Spanish ships and towns. They operated from Jamaica and established a formidable base on the island of Tortuga, off the north coast of San Domingo, the modern Haiti. In 1670, when the English and Spaniards made peace, the Buccaneers were forced to leave their stronghold. Eighteen years later, on the death of their protector Sir Henry Morgan, they abandoned Port Royal, Jamaica, which was destroyed by an earthquake in 1792. Many Buccaneers established themselves in the Bahamas from where they continued their piratical depredations.

Seeking a permanent hiding place for their wealth, several captains are supposed to have sailed up the Atlantic to Nova Scotia. Their ranks included adventurers from all nations, one of whom perhaps would have been capable of constructing the impregnable concealment. Some credence is given to the theory by the words of the West Indian historian, Frederick A. Ober (*The Islands of the Caribbean*, New York, 1904), who states that, at Tortuga, the Buccaneers 'dug deep caves, hollowing out lateral tunnels and blasting holes'.

In 1966 I attempted to assess the engineering capabilities of these Buccaneers. Mr A. Elgar, of the British Embassy at Port-au-Prince, Haiti, wrote: 'As far as I am aware there are absolutely no buildings or ruins or fortifications and the like that are now existing from the pirate period. I myself visited the Ile de la Tortue about six months ago and made enquiries as to the evidence of any ruins of the period but was told that nothing remains. I have also spoken to people who have visited the bay where the pirates used to anchor and they confirm the absence of ruins.' Mr Elgar suggested that I should write to the Reverend Pére Roger Riou, who was said to possess books about Tortuga and its old-time pirates but he was unable to help me. Miss Gloria Robertson, Acting-Librarian at the West Indian Reference Library, Kingston, Jamaica, provided an answer to my query: 'We have consulted Dr D. J. Buisseret of the History Department of the University of the West Indies who has done considerable research on the fortifications in the West Indies. It is Dr Buisseret's opinion that 'deep tunnelling and mining' was not very probable, though he thinks it quite likely that someone like [Sir Henry] Morgan could have had a "genius" who knew about fortifications. However, he had no information on such a person.'

It is unlikely that the Buccaneers would have sailed 2,000 miles to reach Oak Island. Yet it is curious that their exodus from Tortuga coincides with the date noted on the Kidd charts.

Despite the tradition that Mahone Bay was once the haunt of pirates, I reject belief in the Pit's pirate-origin. Their heyday in the Atlantic and Caribbean was over by 1740. Few are likely to have amassed any great wealth, and fewer still would have wished to conceal it. They were notorious spendthrifts. They navigated small vessels, insufficiently armed to overcome towering Spanish galleons, the only source of great loot at sea. The association of pirates and buried treasure is fictional: though admittedly sparse, the records make no mention of concealments and pirate organization operated against such an undertaking, the crews being recruited on a 'no prey no pay' basis. The captain, elected by free vote, took two shares to the crewman's one and had he won a great prize, it is unlikely that he could have persuaded his crew to dig and tunnel for months to create a permanent bank, the spoils of which few might live to enjoy. The magnitude and permanent nature of the Oak Island concealment is foreign to pirate psychology.

Some pirate deposits have been found. In 1933 the English explorer, Frederick Mitchell-Hedges discovered five chests of treasure on the island of Roatan in the Gulf of Honduras which may have been buried in the cave by Sir Henry Morgan, the Buccaneer, following the sack of Panama City in 1671. (Lord Kilbracken, London *Evening Standard*, 8/12 March 1957.) An iron-bound chest, secreted by Blackbeard Teach in the sands of Plum Island, Beaufort County, North Carolina, was found in 1928 (Charles B. Driscoll, *Doubloons*, 1931). It is advisable to remark, as several correspondents have pointed out, that a construction, which may be similar to the Money Pit, exists in the Seychelles Islands in the Indian Ocean, where a treasure hunt has been in progress for many years.

If the Money Pit was dug by pirates it means that it, and its defensive works, were created by unknown pirates, who had amassed considerable loot, the loss of which is unrecorded. It is equally difficult to attribute the works to the French pirates at La Have, forty miles down the coast from Mahone Bay. They were smallfry who preyed upon New England's coastal trade about 1700.

Two other well-established theories require mention. Some investigators believe the island's engineering works were constructed by the crew of a French pay-ship which escaped in 1758 from the siege of Louisburg, the French fortress of Cape Breton Island, 250 miles north of Mahone Bay. The vessel broke through the British blockade, carrying most of the two million pounds sent from France to pay for the rebuilding of the fortress – work that had not been done. Fearing to carry the money back across the Atlantic, the French captain concealed it on Oak Island. But why did he construct such a formidable defence? He needed only to hide the money temporarily while he returned to France for help.

In a variation of this story, another French pay-ship took refuge in Mahone Bay, following the storm which scattered the great Armada of 1748. The Duc d'Anville brought his fleet from France to recapture Louisburg. Several vessels took refuge in Chebucto Bay, the ancient name for Halifax.

According to yet another theory, a Spanish plate-ship on the homeward voyage from the Caribbean became wrecked on the Nova Scotian coast, or was too disabled to continue the voyage. Alternatively her captain may have put in to Mahone Bay in order to loot and conceal her precious cargo. The theory of Spanish origin appears to fulfil several of the required conditions. In the sixteenth and seventeenth centuries the Spanish colonies in Central and South America were the only sources of great mineral wealth. Their plate-fleets, the *flotas* as they were called, sailed high up the North Atlantic, beyond Bermuda, before turning eastwards towards Spain.

C. H. Haring (*Trade and Navigation Between Spain and The Indies in the Time of the Hapsburgs*, Harvard University

Press, 1918) has collected a mass of information about these plate-fleets derived from the Archives of the Indies at Seville and the Royal Academy of History in Madrid. Much more information may lie unsifted. Perhaps a lone galleon became lost. The *flotas* continued to sail until the early part of the nineteenth century.

There seems to be an overwhelming objection to this theory. A Spanish galleon would not have carried the tools, the many picks and spades, required for its crew to have undertaken the work. The men who constructed the Oak Island works came to the island equipped to execute them. They intended to dig and tunnel.

I also reject the remarkable supposition that the Money Pit was dug by a tribe of Incas from Peru, fleeing with their gold from their Spanish masters. Nor can I accept that it was constructed by a party of Norsemen, who may have reached the shores of Nova Scotia about AD 1000. Equally fatuous is the theory that the Pit contains the lost manuscripts of Francis Bacon, the key to the authorship of the Shakespearean plays. Nor need we waste time on the thought that the Pit harbours the jewels of Marie Antoinette, the ill-fated Queen of France. Her jewels were not lost. Her imprisonment and execution took place in 1792-3, two years before the Pit's discovery.

Melbourne Chappell, the soil-owner, possesses a filing cabinet filled with letters from people all over the world, many of whom have advanced their own theories about the Pit's origin. I like best his story of the man who implored a meeting with Chappell should he come to Toronto. Visiting that city, Chappell invited the man to his hotel room. The Pit contained, the man asserted, an inverted, full-scale replica of the Great Pyramid of Egypt and below its apex, in the depths, lay a great treasure. It had been placed there by God Almighty, for the benefit of suffering humanity. In vain Chappell pointed out that the Pit contained earth and not stone. He had great difficulty in getting rid of his visitor, and he had to expel him forcibly.

Gilbert Hedden, the excavator in 1937, believed (as he told me in 1966) that 'the people or person who caused the construction HAD NO INTENTION OF MAKING A RECOVERY IN HIS LIFETIME', and he foresaw, 'the future development of equipment and intelligence to make a recovery effective'.

The many theories about the Pit's origin demonstrate one

remarkable fact – how carefully the depositors had disguised their identity.

It is possible, though the coincidence would be remarkable, that Oak Island was the scene of two independent treasure concealments, one related to the Money Pit and its defensive works, and another made by pirates years before. Anthony Graves, it will be recalled, is reputed to have found coins near his home at Jodrey's Cove. If there were two separate concealments, they had one factor in common, the choice of that particular island. Both parties may have been attracted for the same geological reason, that the island forms a drumlin (a long mound formed by glacial drift) where a deep layer of soil encouraged excavation. It is possible, also, that one party found sink-holes and solution caverns, a feature of limestone formations, which they employed for their concealment. This theory may be supported by the discovery of the Triton Group in 1971, referred to later, of a water-filled cavity at 212 ft.

Discovery of treasure in such a cavity would not, in my opinion, solve the basic problem of Oak Island – the identity of the men who dug the Money Pit and protected it by flooding.

7 Frederick Blair
Collects Legend and Lore

We can now turn our attention to Frederick Leander Blair, a young insurance salesman from the town of Amherst, Nova Scotia. He was born in 1867 and, as a boy, he had heard tales about the Money Pit both from his uncle Isaac and from Jefferson W. McDonald, a member of the 1866 syndicate. Of all the people who had been intrigued by the mystery of Oak Island, Blair was to prove the most patient and careful investigator. He was associated with the operations from 1894 to 1937, and remained keenly interested until his death in 1951. He collected old records diligently and it is largely due to him that we are able to re-create the long history of the operations on the island.

In 1892 Blair was full of enthusiasm and confident that he could recover the treasure of Oak Island. A new syndicate, named the Oak Island Treasure Company, was formed. Frederick Blair was assisted in preparing the Prospectus by Adam A. Tupper, who had been concerned in previous operations. They composed a detailed history of operations on the island. The sum of $60,000 was raised, half of which was used to purchase a three-year lease of the site from the heirs of Anthony Graves. This gave the company the absolute right to retain everything that might be recovered. Only a few hundred shares remained to be sold, stated the second Prospectus, which listed the names of several previous operators who had expressed intention of taking stock in the new company. They included Robert and William Creelman, S. C. Fraser, D. Robinson and Jefferson D. McDonald. A. M. Bridgman of Brockton, Massachusetts, was named President of the company and H. C. Tupper, Treasurer. George E. Houghton of Roxbury, and C. G. L. Moore of Malden, became directors. Full details of the new venture at the now famous treasure hunt site were published by *The Eastern Chronicle* of New Glasgow, on 5 April 1894. The company's intentions and plan of operations were set out in the earlier Prospectus which told prospective investors:

> It is perfectly obvious that the great mistake thus far has been in attempting to 'bail out' the ocean through the various pits. The present Company intends to use the best modern appliances for cutting off the flow of water through the tunnel at some point near the shore, before attempting to pump out the water. It believes, from investigations already made, that such an attempt will be completely successful, and if it is there can be no trouble in pumping out the Money Pit as dry as when the treasure was first placed there.

A meeting of shareholders was held at Truro on 17 April, when several of them expressed a desire for the appointment of a committee of local men to guide the operations and prevent wastage of money. William Creelman read a paper about the previous operations, drawn up in 1847 by P. S. Hamilton who is otherwise unknown. The meeting was attended by several earlier operators: T. Perley Putman of Onslow, a member of the 1850 syndicate; Robert Creelman, another member of that syndicate; Jonathan B. McCully, a member of the Truro companies; Jefferson W. McDonald, another veteran operator; D. Robinson and H. L. Houghton.

The local committee was composed of Jefferson D. McDonald, T. Perley Putman, William Chappell of Amherst, Frederick Blair, Captain Richard Lowerison, Captain John W. Welling, and Adam B. Tupper. The latter was described as a mining engineer who had been associated with the operations in 1850 and 1863.

The activities of Blair's syndicate were watched, states the *Halifax Chronicle* for June 1894 'by crowds of people every day, Sundays included'. Advertisements of a 'Daily Boat to the Oak Island Treasure Grounds' appeared in several newspapers.

The new adventurers set out to locate the flood tunnel, undermine it and destroy it. To achieve its interception a shaft (No. 12) was sunk thirty ft. eastwards of the Money Pit, at a point estimated to lie eight ft. northwards of the line of the tunnel. At the depth of forty-three ft. water suddenly burst into the shaft. It was assumed that this water was from the seventy-five ft. deep shaft, No. 4, which is, for the first time, described as 'full of water'. It lay at least a hundred ft. to the east of shaft No. 12. This 'stagnant, almost black' water was bailed out of shaft No. 12, and was followed by 'clear salt water' which was also bailed out. It was believed to come from the Money Pit. From where water came *at that depth* defies comprehension, for, at the spot indicated, the flood tunnel must lie at the depth of at least ninety ft.

Finally shaft No. 12 was excavated to fifty-three ft. From that depth a tunnel was driven twenty ft. to the south and then worked upwards to within twenty-four ft. of the surface. It failed to strike the flood tunnel, proving, Blair thought, 'that, while the water had been struck at thirty-five to forty feet, the tunnel was not where it was believed to be'.

Either these operations were nonsensical, or the records are wrong, or have been misinterpreted.

Despairing of being able to trace the course of the flood tunnel for the time being, the new operators, as had their predecessors, turned to the Money Pit itself, the magnet that drew and continues to draw all would-be treasure hunters.

In the late summer of 1894 the old shaft (No. 5), positioned about 135 ft. east of the Money Pit, was reopened. A tunnel was found about thirty ft. down leading towards the Money Pit. This, despite its shallow depth, was thought to be 'possibly the pirate (flood) tunnel itself'. The discovery led the operators to consult James McGinnis, the son of Daniel, one of the original discoverers, who was apparently living on the island. He told the new operators that one of the last acts of the Halifax Company in 1867 had been to construct a substantial platform within the Money Pit, just about high water mark, and covered with earth to the surface. When the 1894 operators failed to find this platform, McGinnis insisted, and he was supported by Henry Sellers, that the location of their excavation was wrong. Despite this advice, Tupper's views prevailed and the operators continued to dig at what seems to have been the wrong spot; a not unlikely possibility when one considers the haphazard way in which operations on Oak Island were invariably conducted.

In the summer of 1897 a water-diviner named Chapman from Medford, Massachusetts, persuaded Blair to test his divining rod on the island. The results were startling. Chapman, states Blair, correctly traced the Halifax tunnels, indicated the line of the flood tunnel, and predicted that it entered the Money Pit at 110 ft. Chapman said, 'there is something in the Pit, mostly at the south-west corner'.

Frederick Blair, his son told me, thought a great deal about the men who had dug the Money Pit. He wondered whether they might have left some clue as to their identity, and how to recover the treasure. Throughout his long venture on Oak Island, which was well publicized throughout Canada and the United States, Blair received communications from many individuals, who claimed to know the secret of the Money Pit.

One story with peculiar significance will be discussed later. Another relates how, after pirates had spent considerable time excavating the deep pit and driving long underground tunnels to let in the sea, they were captured by two English frigates which carried them home where they were either hanged or sentenced to gaol. However, one of the crew, a slow-witted man, was spared, and years afterwards while at Bristol gave a sketch of the site to a young sailor who passed it on to a young Halifax pilot. He in turn gave it to his grandson who lived in Boston.

This story, like many other later stories, shows the great interest aroused by the Money Pit, which became, from the turn of the century onwards, a favourite theme for the many weekly and monthly periodicals of the time. A typical example of these effusions, written by Josephine Fredea of Chester, Nova Scotia, which appeared in *Collier's Magazine* (23 September 1905), was reprinted and enlarged in the pamphlet issued by the Chester Board of Trade in 1917. It is worth quoting in full:

> With the hope of securing such prizes to inflame their avarice, it is small wonder that a horde of lawless and adventurous spirits of many nationalities were soon sailing under the black flag. The last Will and testament of one of these men has been recently discovered by a gentleman prominent in English literary circles.
>
> This gentleman, whose name I am not at liberty to disclose, recently purchased an old manor house located near a certain seaport in England. Rambling over his new property he one day visited a long-unused room, where the dust lay thick on floor and furniture. His attention was attracted to an old oaken chest covered with quaint carvings. This he opened and discovered within clothing, nautical instruments and a casket containing a considerable sum of money, several

old maps or charts and other documents, as well as the last will and testament of their owner.

The testator had obviously been a master mariner, presumably the principal in nefarious transactions, since his will began with a lengthy prayer for forgiveness for past misdeeds, the text of which left little doubt that on his deathbed his conscience was giving him serious trouble.

Having done his best (on paper) to introduce himself favourably to the Great Judge before Whom he was shortly to appear, he proceeded to bequeath to his son 'then on the high seas', all the property and money of which he died possessed including the casket of letters and diagrams containing instructions as to the location of certain hidden property.

The significant fact that the old sea chest had lain there undisturbed for so many years, since the clothing, nautical instruments and money were all of ancient date, induced the finder to sift the matter thoroughly. Investigation shows that about the year 1780 the testator's son was impressed from a merchant ship into the Navy and was killed in action. After further careful and exhaustive inquiry, the present owner came to the conclusion that the information was of great value and was about to embark on a search for the hidden property when he chanced to read the story of Oak Island in *Collier's Magazine.*

He was immediately struck by its remarkable similarity to a certain island clearly indicated on the chart in his possession. Between this island 'past Sesambre' (Sambre island at the entrance to Halifax port) as it is written on the chart, and a certain islet in the West Indies, there is marked a clearly defined track; and although most of the writing thereon is in Spanish and Dutch, yet it is apparent at a glance that there was a well-travelled path between the two islands mentioned.

Other papers show that a removal and subsequent deposit of seven packages took place on certain dates, each package bearing separate symbols and initials.

There is also a diagram of the Cove on Oak Island, in the form of a Dutch tobacco pipe, and to this diagram is attached a paper which has not been easy to decipher.

Members of different companies engaged in excavation work on Oak Island, always believed that documents were in existence which would make plain the mystery of the island, and the discovery of the old sea chest shows that their opinions were correct.

'I am not at liberty to go more fully into a description of these documents, for reasons which must be at once apparent to you, but, when peace has at last been concluded and men once more take up the prosaic routine of daily life, some adventurous spirit will no doubt resume the search on Oak Island and finally solve for us its fascinating mystery.

Doubtful as he must have been of the authenticity of these claimed guides to Oak Island, Blair preserved them amongst the records of the Money Pit to which he was now able to add those of the first year of his own unsuccessful operations. As the New Year dawned, Blair, the diligent historian, could not have missed the significance of its date. The approaching summer would herald the hundredth anniversary of the Money Pit's discovery. One hundred years of endeavour had achieved nothing. Overlooked by the island's oak trees, the Money Pit retained its secret. A legend arose about this time that the island would not divulge its secret until the last oak tree had died. If Frederick Blair heard this piece of local lore, he may have watched with interest the ravages of the black ants which had already begun to play havoc amongst the trees.

8 Blair finds a Piece of Parchment and Welling Discovers a Stone Triangle

The year 1895 and most of the following year passed without a renewal of the work on the island. At a meeting held in April 1894, A. S. Lowden, who had been appointed General Manager of the company's operations, outlined his plans to intercept the flood tunnel, look for the hypothetical gate which could control the flood water, and re-tackle the Money Pit itself. An attempt to raise further capital failed, and on 26 November the directors appointed a new Board of Management consisting of T. Perley Putman, George W. Fullerton, W. H. McDonald and William Chappell. Frederick Blair remained as Treasurer. The public were invited to subscribe the further $2,000 required with which to purchase a first class steam pump.

An enlargement of shaft No. 2, which had been sunk in 1805 close to the Money Pit, appears to have been the only major work accomplished in 1896. Then in April 1897, the company attempted to deepen the Money Pit. Reaching the depth of 110 ft., they discovered the inlet of a tunnel, well cribbed and nine ft. square, with salt water in the bottom. This tunnel seems to have entered the Money Pit above the flood tunnel. Digging upwards the workmen discovered a well-built platform which meant that they were in the shaft sunk by the Halifax Company in 1866, James McGinnis and Henry Sellers having questioned its exact location. The shaft was carried upwards to ground-level, the workmen hoisting out or repairing the old cribbing, much of which was out of alignment and askew. Confirmation that they were indeed within the original Money Pit came when the workmen reaching the depth of 111 ft., discovered a well-defined opening at the side of the shaft, two and a half ft. wide, and filled with stones, gravel and sand. The sea poured through this opening with great force and pressure, indicating that the inlet of the flood tunnel, located previously by the Halifax men, had again been found. The sides of the tunnel were smooth and perpendicular and had been cut through firm clay; the roof was square across and the whole tunnel was well constructed.

The water in the tunnel rose rapidly because of the failure of the pumping system and the men were driven from the pit.

Readers may wonder why, having located the flood tunnel's inlet, the operators did not attempt to plug it, and so free the Money Pit from flooding. This was impossible. because the pressure of the water, forced downwards by the tides of the ocean, would have ejected any plug, however substantial.

The management Committee decided that it would be less expensive to stop the flow of water from the shore, by tracing and blocking its inlet, than to pump it from the Money Pit. In an attempt to locate the inlet, borings were made at Smith's Cove, about fifty ft. above high water mark and along a line at right angles to the supposed course of the tunnel. The diagram drawn of these operations still survives and it shows that five borings, each five in. in diameter, were made to 95, 90, 80, 90 and 95 ft. reading from south-east to north-west. No water was encountered in borings, 1, 2, 4 and 5, and charges of dynamite produced no apparent result. But salt water and rocks were struck at eighty ft. in boring No. 3. The water rose to tide level and ebbed and flowed with the tide. It was assumed that this central boring had punctured the flood tunnel and a charge of 160 pounds of dynamite was lowered and detonated. Observers stationed at the Money Pit reported that the water therein boiled and foamed for some time, thus establishing a connection between Pit and bore hole. Believing that the flood tunnel had at last been blocked, the syndicate returned to work at the Money Pit.

The discovery of the course of the tunnel close to the shore at Smith's Cove, indicates that the flood tunnel lay at the depth of eighty ft. within fifty ft. of the shore. It could not, therefore, have been the source of the water which had been found in shafts Nos. 4 and 5, one of which had been sunk to seventy-five ft., and the other to a mere thirty-five ft. Also the depth at which the tunnel was found, within fifty ft. of high water mark, indicates that the sump hole, into which the fan-drains built beneath the monster sponge constructed on the beach converged, must have been about seventy ft. deep.

The operators considered that the cache they were seeking had formerly lain at the depth of ninety-eight ft. and that the oaken chests had dropped into the void beneath following the great collapse.

Resuming their operations at the Money Pit, the hopeful treasure seekers decided to make several borings, by means of a two and a half inch drill placed within a three inch pipe. Blair carefully noted their locations, confirmed in a statement by William Chappell. Despite the dynamiting near the shore, the Money Pit remained flooded to within thirty-three ft. of the surface. (The significance of this fact will be revealed later.) The water was pumped out to the ninety ft. level where a drilling platform was rigged to enable the borings to cover as large an area as possible.

William Chappell described these borings in a sworn statement:

Several holes (more than three) were bored, and this statement is a composite report of all holes drilled except in so far as is necessary to give a clear, succinct and easily understood history of the work. Most of the drilling was done in loose or soft and what appeared to be disturbed ground; blue clay was encountered between 130 and 151 feet and also between 160 and 171 feet. In one hole we appeared to be in the channel in which the water was coming up and being pumped out at the rate of about 400 gallons per minute. It was the generally disturbed and loose conditions, and the blue clay, that induced the workmen to drill their first hole below 130 feet.

Wood was struck at 122 feet and at 126 feet and deeper as stated herein. Iron was encountered at 126 feet in one hole, and it stopped the pipe. The pipe proved to be on the edge of iron, but efforts made to drive it past resulted in failure.

A 1½" drill was put down past the obstruction and it went through the blue clay to 151 feet and struck what appeared to be a soft stone. Cuttings of this stone when compared, looked just like cement, and as analytical chemists subsequently pronounced samples from this material to have the composition of cement, it is hereafter referred to as cement. Twenty inches down in this cement, we struck wood, a few chips from which were brought up. An auger was substituted for the drill and five inches of oak wood were bored through.

When the auger passed through the wood it dropped from one and one half to two inches and rested upon a substance the character of which no person would attempt to state. After considerable twisting of the auger on the substance, it was carefully withdrawn and the borings brought up therewith were preserved by Mr Putman. The drill was then again put down when we found we were apparently on soft metal that could be moved slightly thereby forming a crevice or space into which the drill, when in alignment, would drop and stick or wedge. This happened a number of times and it was often necessary to pry the drill loose. After working for two hours or more, we managed to get down four inches when the drill worked easier, but it would not go down under the ordinary method of drilling (raising and dropping the rods) but by a continuous twisting and turning of the rods under constant pressure, we managed to get 18 or 20 inches deeper, a total of 24 inches of material bored through under the wood. The drill then struck a substance similar to that encountered immediately under the wood. No special effort was made to get through this.

In working down the twenty inches, the space made by the drill would fill at once under the tool as it was raised, and it would fill up nearly the whole twenty inches when the rods were raised that much. We worked over five hours in getting down the foot, and the drill came up as sharp as it went down.

'The conclusion was that the first four inches consisted of metal in bars which were pushed aside by the drill enough to permit it to pass, and that the additional twenty inches consisted of coin or metal in small pieces that fell into the space left by the tool as it was drawn up, and also that under these small pieces there was more metal (not iron) in bars.

It was at once decided to secure this drill hole by piping below 126 feet and then to obtain a sample of the small metal pieces. To that end, a $1\frac{1}{2}''$ pipe was lowered through the $3''$ pipe and forced past the iron obstruction at 126 feet. It was discovered, however, that this construction had turned the small pipe from its course and it struck hard ground, supposed to be the wall of the pit, instead of going down to the cement.

The $1\frac{1}{2}''$ pipe was then withdrawn and the drill again lowered through the larger pipe, but it followed the hole made by the small pipe below 126 feet and the hole to the cement was thereby lost. When the $1\frac{1}{2}''$ pipe was withdrawn it was found that in forcing it past the obstruction at 126 feet, a V shaped piece extending for about one third of the circumference of the pipe at the lower end and up about three inches, had been cut out.

The three inch pipe was then reset and another hole drilled, and the pipe put down until it rested solidly upon the cement. At 153 feet we apparently touched wood on one side which extended down about four feet, the cement extending about three feet further to a depth of approximately 160 feet, with a total thickness of about seven feet from top of wood to bottom of cement.

We then bored into a quite firm blue clay possessing the characteristics of puddled clay. This extended down to 171 feet where iron was struck. The iron was very solid and the metallic sound could be plainly heard at the surface. We drilled on it two hours or more, getting into it not more than one quarter inch. The drill was taken out, sharpened and tempered for iron and two more hours were spent in drilling and getting down another quarter-inch. The drill showed no wear when withdrawn, it was given a few raps on stone which took the edge off. The clay and material at the bottom of the hole were brought up with a sand pump. A magnet was run through this material and it loaded up with fine iron cuttings thereby producing conclusive proof that it was iron we had been drilling on at 171 feet. No further attempt was made to go through this iron.

It has been accepted, and still is by some investigators, that the information obtained from these borings establishes the existence, in the depths of the Money Pit, of a wood and iron chamber, sealed and rendered water-tight by a casing of cement. A chamber thirteen ft. wide and twenty ft. deep, filled with coins and gold bars! But, if the depositors had constructed such a treasure chamber, why had they placed two chests at ninety-eight ft.? The existence, real or imaginary, of one cache seemed to deny the likelihood of the other. The eager treasure seekers found no difficulty in supplying a convincing answer: the chests were a decoy. Anyone reaching them would conclude that they had found the treasure. They would depart rejoicing and would not seek its real bulk farther down.

William Chappell failed to remark two discoveries which were noted by Blair. In one boring the auger brought up a small round object, which was later identified as parchment. In another, the drill entered a channel at the depth of

126 ft. from where water spouted up the pipe at the rate of 400 gallons a minute. The drillers concluded that this violent rush of water indicated the existence of a second flood tunnel into the Money Pit which came probably from the south shore of the island, rather than from Smith's Cove.

Two flood tunnels! The treasure so safeguarded *must* be immense!

Samples of the substance thought to be cement were sent to England in 1897 for analysis by the famous firm of industrial chemists, A. Boake Roberts. In their report they stated that they found the two stones to be of the following composition:

	No. 1	No. 2
Lime (CaC)	37.40%	37.18%
Carbonate (CO 2)	33.20%	34.00%
Silicas (SiC 2)	13.20%	13.92%
Iron and Alumina (Fe 203 or A 1203)	10.19%	10.13%
Moisture (at 120°C)	0.34%	0.29%
Magnesium &c.	5.67%	4.48%
	100.00	100.00

When invited to state whether they considered these stones to be artificial or natural, A. Boake Roberts said that 'while it is impossible to state definitely, we are of the opinion that it is cement which has been worked by hand'.

Blair and his associates believed that the discovery of the tiny ball of parchment brought up from the depths by the drilling constituted irrefutable proof that the Money Pit contained treasure. It was found amongst several chips of wood which were examined under the microscope in the presence of a number of men who gathered in the courthouse, by Dr A. E. Porter of Amherst, to whom the result of the boring had been brought by Putman. A compact ball, about the size of a grain of rice, with fuzz or short hair on the surface was found among the borings. In the words of the Affidavit made by Dr Porter on 6 September 1897, when flattened out it seemed to be 'parchment and that certain marks on it had the appearance of being written with ink and part of some word'. A photograph revealed the letters to be 'V.I.' but it could not be determined what language they represented. This piece of parchment has survived in the possession of M. R. Chappell of Sydney, Nova Scotia.

'This piece of parchment,' stated Frederick Blair in an interview reported by the Toronto *Telegram* on 22 April 1930, 'is more convincing evidence of buried treasure than a few doubloons would be. I am satisfied that either treasure of immense value or priceless historical documents are in a chest at the bottom of the Pit.'

The treasure hunters were so excited by these discoveries, that they decided to finance future operations themslves rather than to offer shares to the public. They now embarked upon a fresh enterprise: nothing less than the sinking of a new shaft (No. 14) to a depth of 200 ft., forty ft. south of the Pit, the object being to intercept the second and lower water inlet into the Money Pit. The workmen dug to 112 ft. without encountering water and three ft. farther down they came upon an old tunnel which was identified as one of those made by the Halifax Company. A rush of salt water drove them from the new shaft.

Undaunted by this setback, in the spring of 1898 the treasure seekers sunk yet another shaft (No. 15) thirty-five ft. south-west of the previous shaft (No. 14) and about eighty ft. from the Money Pit. At the 105 ft. level an old dry tunnel was encountered which was again attributed to the Halifax Company. At 168 ft. salt water broke into the new shaft on the south-western side through a seam of sand. This shaft was abandoned and four more shafts (Nos. 16, 17, 18 and 19) were sunk to depths of 134, 95, 160 and 144 ft., apparently to the south-east and about a hundred ft. from the Money Pit. They all had to be abandoned because of rushing water. Pumping at the Money Pit, during the sinking of these shafts, held the water level at seventy ft. and it was noted that, when the depth of 160 ft. was reached in shaft No. 15, the water in the Money Pit fell fourteen ft., within an hour. It then rose again, and the water level in the new shaft became equal. Five hours' pumping were required to reduce the level of the water in the Money Pit to seventy ft.

Again the syndicate changed its tactics. It was decided that they should determine whether or not the flood tunnel from Smith's Cove had been blocked effectively, and if another flood tunnel entered the Money Pit below it. Thus a pump was set up on the shore (which shore is not stated but

1. A 1929 survey showing that the eastern end of Oak Island is part of the Windsor Series (limestone, gypsum, sandstone) which extends from N.E. to S.W. across the head of Mahone Bay.

Scale, 1 mile to 1 inch ‒ 1/63360

2. Air view of Oak Island taken in 1943.

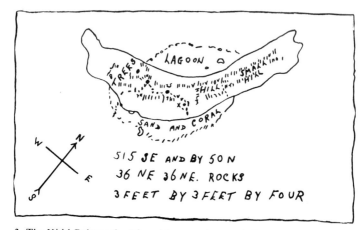

3. The Kidd-Palmer chart found in a sea chest and photographed by the British Museum.

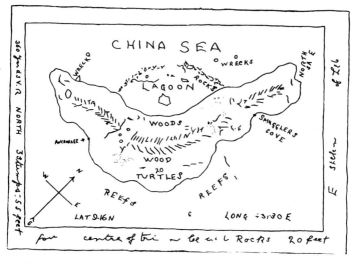

The Kidd-Palmer chart found in "William and Sarah Kidd. Their box." Also photographed by the British Museum. Both these charts show an island that bears some resemblance to Oak Island.

presumably on the south shore), and sea water was pumped into shaft No. 18. Members of the syndicate stationed themselves on the shore to watch for the muddy water which they expected to emerge. It showed itself not at Smith's Cove but at three places far apart on the south shore at about low water mark. This test confirmed that the water course from Smith's Cove had been blocked and provided the startling information that there were also three outlets or inlets on the south shore.

Determined to confirm this information, the syndicate conducted three further tests. They pumped water into the Money Pit; in one hour it had receded by four ft. They refilled it. Next morning the water had receded to tide level, thirty-three ft. Then red dye was put into the water and when the level in the Money Pit receded, the red coloration appeared on the south shore at the same three places as before. Not content with this proof, the active members of the syndicate exploded a charge of dynamite on the south shore; only a few minutes elapsed before muddy water appeared in the Money Pit.

The tests confirmed the existence of a second water course between the Money Pit and the south shore of the island. Whether or not this constituted a man-made tunnel or a natural feature will be discussed later.

These discoveries elated rather than discouraged the treasure hunters. Although they were now convinced that they faced two sources of flooding, they believed that the evidence of the existence of a second, and lower, flood tunnel increased the value of the supposed treasure cache.

They sank a new shaft (No. 20) on the west side, close to or even overlapping the Pit, dividing it with cribbing and encountering the old cribbing of shaft No. 6, made by the Truro Company in 1850. At 118 ft. water surged into this new shaft with a greater force than the pumps could combat. Before the shaft was abandoned, its bottom was identified as being hard soil, ringed by gravel on the eastern side, within which lay a core of clay so soft that it could be handled without the aid of a pick. Borings made to 126 ft. disclosed boulders and clay. They encountered neither iron nor cement.

The company ran out of money. Captain Welling's investment of $4,000 and Putman's of $20,000 had gone; the workmen were clamouring for their wages and, on the distraint of the firm owning the machinery, the company's equipment and assets were sold by the Sheriff. Undaunted by failure, Frederick Blair, using his own money, bought out the other shareholders. By December 1900, he had obtained full control of the company. Writing in October 1898, Blair reaffirmed his confidence in ultimate success:

> When we went to work at the island two years ago, we knew comparatively nothing about conditions as they existed. We supposed at that time that the Money Pit was not over 120 feet deep and that the treasure was not over 110 feet down. Our work has since proved that the Pit is not less than 180 feet deep, that there are two tunnels instead of one, and that one of them is not less than 160 feet down, and that there is treasure at different points in the Pit, from 126 feet down to 170 feet, without a doubt. We have also found out that the work done by the Halifax Company is a greater hindrance to the procuring of the treasure than is the original work.
>
> We now claim that there is nothing that can prevent us getting the treasure, if we succeed in getting a pumping pit down.

One other discovery made at this time must be noted. While exploring the south shore of the island in 1897, Captain John Welling found and pointed out to Blair a large equilateral triangle made of beach stones, hidden in a mass of undergrowth just above high water mark. From its base a vertical arrow of stones ran to its apex. Neither Welling nor Blair could fathom the purpose of this triangle. Its existence was forgotten until it was rediscovered under dramatic circumstances in 1937.

9 Captain Bowdoin Fails to Conquer

By 1903 Frederick Blair's private funds were exhausted and he took no further active part in the operations on the island. In 1905, however, he acquired a long lease from Henry Sellers, owner of the eastern part of Oak Island, and this enabled him to continue to control the situation. He paid an annual rental of $100 during active operations, and $20 a year while the works were idle. He also acquired from the Government of Nova Scotia, the 'right' to seek for treasure on the island for forty years, a period which was later extended by five years to compensate for the years lost between 1939 and 1945.

Blair's 'right' to search may well have been illusory. Possession of the soil of Oak Island did not, and still does not, give the landlord or his lessee the right to search for treasure. That Royal Prerogative had been transferred to the Provincial Government of Nova Scotia which had already informed operators that any treasure found belonged to the Crown: the Government would take a percentage and allow the remainder to those who made the discovery. To cover the position, the Government gave Blair authority under the Mines Act, only allowing him the right to mine for gold or silver in its natural state, but its possession did prevent others from searching on the island. This involved situation was cleared after Blair's death in 1954.

In that year the Nova Scotia Legislative enacted a Statute declaratory of the Crown's prerogative, requiring those who desired to seek for treasure to apply for a licence, to pay damages to the land owner, and to pay a royalty to the Crown. This Treasure Trove Act is incorporated (Chapter 299) in the Revised Statutes of Nova Scotia (1954). (See Appendix C, pages 150-2.) A licence to search for treasure on Oak Island was granted in 1950, and has been renewed annually, to Melbourne R. Chappell of Sydney, Nova Scotia. He is the person to whom enquiries for the right of search on the eastern part of the island should be addressed. The royalty demanded by the Government is, I believe, now fixed at 4%.

These necessary legal matters having been discussed, we can return to consider the new stage of operations. They began, as usual, with high hopes and ended in controversy and vituperation.

The long and unsuccessful search for treasure on Oak Island attracted the attention of an American engineer, Captain Harry L. Bowdoin of New York. He had rich and influential friends, Franklin D. Roosevelt, the future President, among them. Bowdoin's other associates included Albert Gallatin, Duncan E. Harris, Frederick Childs and John W. Shields. Bowdoin announced the plans of his 'Old Gold Salvage Company' on 18 March 1909 in the *New York Herald*. He was described as: '. . . a mining, mechanical and marine engineer, a Master and Pilot and has a licence as a submarine diver. He has dredged harbours and built bridges for the government and for corporations and says that modern machinery and engineering science will solve in a jiffy the difficulties Captain Kidd made to guard his treasure.'

The article continued:

> Captain Bowdoin stated that he has procured a mining licence under which he will be compelled to pay two per cent of any treasure he finds to the Dominion Government. Henry Sellers owns Oak Island and Frederick L. Blair of Amherst, Nova Scotia, has a lease of it. With them Mr Bowdoin has made a contract he says, for the apportionment of that ten million dollars and he has ordered such machinery as he will need. He plans to start with a crew of six men on May 1st going by rail. His machinery he will ship in a chartered schooner. The maximum outlay he estimates at $15,000.
>
> 'Any competent engineer could clear up that affair in no time', he said yesterday. 'And I don't want more than two weeks for the work, after I get my machinery and crew on the ground. It will be a vacation and about all I stand to lose is the wages of my men and my own time, for the machinery will be valuable in my business afterwards. I am not going to organise any company, though I may take a personal friend or two into the enterprise.'

But on the same day another interview given to the *New York Times*, declared that: 'He had not yet decided how he will get the treasure as he may sink a caisson down around the place where the treasure is supposed to be, or may build another jetty. He may even send a diver down in one of the holes, equipped with a pick-axe. He has never been to Oak Island, so he will have to decide on that when he gets there.'

Bowdoin formed a company, with the registered directors: Captain H. L. Bowdoin, President; F. L. Blair, Vice-President; and two American directors, Attorney L. H. Andrews and accountant G. D. Mosher. The company's authorized capital of $250,000 was divided into shares of one dollar each. and a lease was negotiated with Blair to last until 1 September 1910.

The company's Prospectus outlined Bowdoin's grandiose plans:

Over one hundred years ago a treasure, estimated to be over ten million dollars, was buried on Oak Island, in Mahone Bay, Nova Scotia, supposedly by pirates, who took such pains to safeguard it that, although numerous attempts have been made to recover it, it lies undisturbed to this day. These failures were due to lack of modern machinery and ignorance; each expedition being stopped by water and lack of funds. The pirates connected the pit in which the treasure was buried with the ocean by an underground tunnel, so that when buried and the tunnel opened the water level was six feet above the treasure. The diggers in the pit, which is quite a distance from the shore, have invariably been driven out by this water, which is salt, and rises and falls with the tide. As a pit was dug near the Money Pit one hundred and ten feet deep without striking any water, yet became flooded when they tunnelled into the Money Pit, it proves the existence of an underground connection between the pit and the ocean. The location of this tunnel has been practically determined, but as yet no one has known how to cut it off.

That there really is some sort of treasure there has been verified by gold shavings and part of a watch chain brought up with borings from the crude implements used. Since these borings were made, the parties have made regular payments on a lease of the property, which gives them the exclusive right to any treasure that may be found, which lease has been fully augmented by a Government permit.

69

Believing from the above, and from other facts, that a treasure of some value is buried in the pit on Oak Island, Nova Scotia, and knowing that with modern methods of machinery the recovery of that treasure is easy, ridiculously easy, an exclusive contract has been entered into with the owners and leaseholders of the property for its recovery.

There are several methods which may be employed in the recovery of the treasure, a simple one being as follows: A core drill, bringing up a continuous core 2 inches in diameter of the material bored through, will be used to locate the treasure, then a series of holes will be bored parallel with and near the shore and across the tunnel. When the tunnel is definitely located, sheet piling will be driven across it. An 'orange peel' bucket 1¼ yards capacity, will be put to work and a hole dug between the sheet piling and the shore into and through the tunnel. A hole will then be dug back of the sheet piling and into the tunnel, and the water pumped out; if not entirely tight another 'plug' can be put in at the water's edge. The bucket will then be moved to the pit and dig the dirt out of the same at the rate of 1½ cubic yards or more per minute. This bucket does, of course, work equally well through and under water (as in a dredge boat), and will take hold of and bring up anything that it can span – 7 feet 3 inches. However, as soon as there is sufficient water in the pit a centrifugal turbine pump, capable of lifting one thousand gallons per minute – one hundred and fifty feet vertically – will be lowered into the pit from a derrick and the water pumped out. If the tunnel plugs have done their work, the pump will clear out the water; the treasure be easily recovered, and all underground workings explored.

Should, however, the tunnel not be located; the pump not be able to keep out the water, and the bucket not bring up all of the treasure, some, perhaps, having slipped to one side, then, and in that event one of 'Bowdoin's Air Lock Caissons' could be placed in the pit, sunk through water or earth to any depth desired, and side tubes forced out to reach any direct spot. Compressed air keeps out all water and allows men to work at the bottom, and send any articles up and through the air lock. The caisson is now used in sinking foundations through earth and water to bed rock; for foundations of buildings and through the water of a river and to bed rock beneath its bed, for foundations for bridges, piers etc. The treasure can positively be recovered by its use.

The wide publicity given by the press of the intention of Mr Bowdoin to recover this Oak Island Treasure has resulted in the receipt of a number of letters calling attention to other treasures and valuables that could be recovered through scientific modern equipment. Several of these are of exceptional interest, being valuable, non-perishable cargoes of vessels, and sunken valuables, the locations of which are known.

As no systematic, scientific efforts have been made to recover and salvage the more or less valuable cargoes etc. of wreck which are piling up at the rate of over one hundred a year, it is deemed good business policy to get together a complete modern equipment, and after the recovery of the treasure at Oak Island, to utilise said equipment in a general salvage and wrecking business.

To this end the Old Gold Salvage and Wrecking Company has been formed, and has taken up the matter on a *cold, business basis*. The objects of the Company are:

...*First:* To recover, by use of modern methods, the Ten Million Dollars buried on Oak Island, Nova Scotia.

Second: To then use the machinery and equipment purchased for the salvage and wrecking of sunken vessels known to contain gold and valuable cargo.

The lease and government permit, under which the recovery of the treasure will be made, are now controlled by the Company.

The officers and directors of the Company are practical men; well versed in pneumatic and general wrecking operations; who will be on the ground and superintend operations for the recovery of the treasure.

The recovery of the treasure would yield a dividend 1,000 per cent on the entire capital stock, and, as operations should begin in May or June and be completed in three or four weeks, should be available this summer. This will leave for the salvage of an exceptionally valuable cargo next winter, when the plant would operate in southern waters where certain other valuables await our attention. To purchase the equipment, stock is now offered to the general public at a popular price, $1.00 per share. No order for less than ten shares will be accepted.

Bowdoin and his men duly arrived on Oak Island in August 1909. Franklin Roosevelt, who had not yet become stricken with paralysis, paid at least one visit to the island. Bowdoin facetiously named his headquarters 'Camp Kidd', and inscribed a stone, 'In Memory of Captain Kidd'. Finding two shafts side by side (the combined shaft sunk in 1899) Bowdoin cleaned out one, which was flooded to tide level, strengthened the cribbing and secured the platform which had been used for the drilling operations in 1898. He pumped the water out of the Money Pit and removed the platforms, connected by ladders, which had been placed at each ten ft. level to a depth of 107 ft. A diver reported that the cribbing was in a dangerous state below that level and that the bottom was covered by planks and pieces of timber. The Money Pit was then cleared to the depth of 113 ft. Convinced he was directly above the treasure, Bowdoin put down a core-drill.

The drill descended through sixteen ft. of gravel and sand, sixteen ft. of blue clay, stones and sand, and brought up traces of what was believed to be cement from 149 ft. Excitement mounted when the drill bored through what appeared to be a casing of solid cement, which they believed enclosed the treasure chest or chamber. The drill penetrated only yellow clay and stones for the next eighteen ft. It reached bedrock at 167 ft. Twenty-five further borings, to depths of between 155 and 171 ft., revealed no trace of either chests or chamber. A resident of Chester, J. B. Thompson, who was present, told Blair that he had seen, embedded in the core-drill, a thin disc of metal, bright on one side.

The 'cement' found in the Money Pit was submitted for testing by Captain Bowdoin to Columbia University where Professors Chandler, Kemp and Woolson reported it to be 'natural limestone pitted by the action of water'.

On completion of the season's work, Bowdoin applied to Blair for an extension of his lease until 1 January 1912, being determined 'not to quit without another try'. Blair insisted that Bowdoin must first show that 'he had sufficient funds on hand, or at his disposal, to complete the work in the proper manner'. Annoyed by Blair's lack of confidence, Bowdoin threatened that, if the extension was not granted, he would make a report that would not help in getting further investment for exploration on Oak Island in the future.

On his return to New York, Bowdoin published an article in *Collier's Magazine* (18 August 1911) entitled *Solving the Mystery of Oak Island*. He claimed that 'there never was a pirate or any other treasure in the Money Pit on Oak Island' and asserted that, if a subterranean tunnel had been required, one could have been built only 150 feet in length from the south shore to the Pit, rather than the tremendous operation required from Smith's Cove. He claimed that the sea reached the Money Pit by percolating through the soil. Blair replied to Bowdoin's attack in an article which was published in the Amherst *Daily News* on 23 February 1912. To Bowdoin's charge that the Money Pit had been 'salted' with the piece of parchment in order to sell stock, Blair patiently recapitulated the facts, pointing out that following its discovery 'nearly all the funds were put up by insiders'.

During the year 1911 Oak Island was inspected by the geologist Rudolph Faribault. He expressed the opinion that the original depressions which encouraged the search for treasure, must have been sink-holes, a geological feature found frequently in limestone formations of which the eastern end of Oak Island consisted. Faribault's report was printed in an official publication. It escaped the notice of the Oak Island adventurers until 1965, when belief in the sink-hole theory was revived by J. Gwynne Evans, an Englishman who visited the island that summer.

10 No Lack of Adventurers

After a century of haphazard digging, the eastern part of Oak Island had become pocked by a labyrinth of shafts, twenty all told, and undermined by a maze of tunnels extending in unknown directions. The Money Pit had become a morass of puddled mud, continually re-saturated by the water which surged in at each high tide. At the conclusion of each attempt to pump it out, it refilled the Pit to tide level. Without exact knowledge of the operations of their predecessors, each eager syndicate was forced to start afresh.

In 1912, a new method for overcoming the difficulties encountered by the early explorers was suggested. Professor S. A. Williams of Soldier's Grove, Wisconsin, advocated the use of the Pootach freezing process to stabilize the quicksand of watery mud that lay deep within the Money Pit. This process had been publicized in the *Scientific American Supplement* of 25 May 1895. Captain John Welling, who had been concerned in previous operations, appears to have been associated with Williams who incorporated the Oak Island Salvage Company in Wisconsin with an authorized capital of $20,000. Half the stock was offered to the public.

Professor Williams proposed to sink thirty-five holes, each five in. in diameter and three ft. apart, to a depth of 160 ft., enclosing the Money Pit. These holes would be pumped dry and filled with the freezing mixture, formed of calcium chloride at a temperature of thirty-five degrees below zero. It would be kept circulating by means of small pipes inside the casings. The slush at the bottom of the Money Pit would be frozen and a ring of ice created round its base. According to Thomas P. Leary (*The Oak Island Enigma*, privately printed, Omaha, Nebraska, 1953) Professor Williams also proposed to sink a steel caisson, kept under air pressure to prevent the water from rising, and lowered by firing a charge of dynamite below ground. The Company's Prospectus stated that 'within a week after beginning the work we expect to recover a part of the treasure so that the stockholders will know definitely what to expect'.

The project, however, never materialized.

Following the failure of this enterprise, Frederick Blair was approached with an offer from William S. Lozier, an engineer from Rochester, New York. He contracted with the firm of Sprague and Henwood of Scranton, Pennsylvania, to carry out certain drilling operations within and close to the Money Pit, and to make exact measurements of the area. No new discoveries were made, but these measurements later proved valuable in re-locating the exact site of the Money Pit which, in Blair's opinion, had become lost. In November 1920, Blair informed an enquirer that 'the Pit caved in and more or less filled up with cribbing, the timbers being in every imaginable shape. The ground surrounding the Pit has also caved in more or less and the spaces in and around the Pit are full of water.' The true site of the Money Pit was not re-located, in Blair's opinion, until 1936.

Another optimistic adventurer turned up in August 1921. This man, Edward W. Bowne, an engineer from Newark, New Jersey, planned to sink a shaft six ft. by six ft., fifteen ft. from the Money Pit. Tunnels would then be driven at various depths to recover the boxes of treasure which 'could be located by sounding with an iron rod after the proper depth is reached'. When, after five weeks' work, nothing had been achieved, Blair terminated the agreement, and received $1,000 compensation by arbitration.

Between 1922 and 1931 Blair tried to find a wealthy man who would be willing to invest $50,000 in the recovery of the treasure. His advertisements, one of which appeared in the *Journal of Commerce*, Boston, on 7 December 1922, attracted no interest other than an editorial comment 'Can Buried Treasure Lure Wall Street?' and themes for the articles about Oak Island and its fabulous cache of gold which continued to appear regularly in many American and Canadian periodicals.

In 1931 William Chappell, who had taken part in Blair's first venture in 1894, and who had operated the drill when the piece of parchment was found, returned to the scene with his brother, Renwick R. Chappell. Blair accompanied William Chappell to Oak Island and the work was re-started. Where exactly did the original Money Pit lie? Chappell identified the site from the crib work he himself had built in 1897. Blair preferred a spot slightly to the north and east. Despite this disagreement it was decided to sink a new shaft (No. 21) which became known as the 'Chappell' shaft, twelve ft. by fourteen ft. to the south-west of the shaft excavated in 1897, and also to enclose shaft No. 12. As the digging proceeded, evidence of early operations came to light: at 127 ft., a pick; at 123 ft., an axe head, resembling an Acadian axe, and estimated to be 250 years old, its edge tempered and not rusted, although the rest of it was badly corroded; at 116 ft., an anchor fluke, a bit of oak under a piece of granite, measuring four ft. by four ft., and which needed to be broken by blasting; at 127 ft., part of a miner's seal-oil lamp, and at 130 ft. and 150 ft., further pieces of granite.

These discoveries perplexed Blair, who recorded his thoughts:

From 116 ft. six in. to 155 ft., the earth in over half of the shaft was much disturbed. How these articles reached a depth of from ten to seventeen ft. lower than any searcher ever reached, is a question that must be answered.

These tools, I believe, belonged to searchers who worked there many years ago, and had fallen from a much higher level to where found. Both [the axe and the pick] were in perpendicular position and in soft, disturbed or filled ground.

The only reply that I can think of is that there existed an open space into which they fell when the Pit collapsed years ago, and at that time the Pit had been opened only to eighty-six ft., hence these tools may have fallen as much as thirty-five ft. or more.

At about 150 ft. we commenced to uncover broken-up pieces of stone, the nature of which no person here can identify. They have the appearance of the so-called cement which was drilled through in previous years, and yet it does not resemble it in all respects. These stones first appeared in the disturbed portion of the Pit, a chunk or two, and gradually spread over the whole area.

As the men worked deeper, the bottom became largely covered with this stuff in broken pieces, and Mr Stevenson, the miner in charge of the actual work, says they appear just as if they had been dumped or dropped from a higher point. At the present level, the bottom of the Pit is covered with this stuff, and it seems as if we are in a bed of it that may extend considerably deeper. The water comes through under the shoe at the bottom on one side, and a few feet up the wall as well as at the bottom on the opposite side.

The question now is, where is the wood and treasure – metal in pieces – which dropped from 100 ft., the iron struck at

126 ft. by drillers, the cement and wood drilled into between 153 and 157 ft., and the iron at 171 ft.? It appears as if we had gone past them. They certainly must be somewhere in the near vicinity of our Pit.

It has been the theory of many connected with previous expeditions, that there was an open chamber below the deposit at 100 ft., and this deposit fell into the chamber when the Money Pit collapsed years ago. There was certainly an open space of some description under that deposit, otherwise the result of the collapse would never have been so great a drop, if any collapse had occurred.

I am convinced that down to 150 feet at least, one end of our pit was over the edge of what was once an open chamber. Due to the collapse of supports, etc. above, this chamber has been filled with broken ground or clay, through which the water being pumped has passed. Tons and tons of clay have passed out with the water this summer, and the gravel and other solids keep settling down to solid bottom as the work progresses. The wall of this chamber, undermined possibly by the water, has broken down in the vicinity of our pit, and perhaps it is some of that wall we have taken out.

That is my theory. We certainly have a vast treasure here, and it will possibly require as much work to recover it all as we have already done.

The Chappell shaft (No. 21) reached a depth of 163½ ft. Lateral holes were driven at various levels and in all directions, and three tunnels were driven from the bottom. Neither these holes or tunnels, nor the drillings made into the bottom of the shaft, disclosed anything new. William Chappell, who had spent some $50,000, discontinued his operations in 1932.

Further drilling in the Money Pit was undertaken in 1932 by a New York engineer, John Talbot, on behalf of Miss Mary B. Stewart who headed a group of financiers. Talbot drilled for seven weeks at a point seven ft. from the northern corner of shaft No. 21 to the depth of 150 ft. He found nothing.

On 16 September 1933 Blair made an agreement with Thomas M. Nixon of Victoria, British Columbia, who formed the Canadian Oak Island Treasure Company with an authorized capital of $225,000. Half that amount of stock was offered to the public, who, however, failed to respond to the enticing bait. Nixon believed that the treasure had been deposited on Oak Island by 'a tribe of Incas who had fled from Mexico' (the Incas lived in Peru), hundreds of years ago, carrying jewels and precious metals. They had buried their riches in a deep tunnel, running from the Atlantic ocean to the centre of the island, and had then vanished. Nixon advanced his theory that 'the principal treasure had been deposited at the bottom of the Pit and sealed. Another deposit, formed of several oak, iron-bound chests, had been made above it, to throw any possible discoverer off the scent and persuade him he had found all the treasure.' Gates had been placed in the flood tunnels to shut off the sea water and permit entrance to the treasure chamber.

Nixon intended to drive down a circle of interlocking steel pilings, forming a huge caisson to enclose the Money Pit to the depth necessary to recover the treasure. But instead of undertaking this costly operation, he spent the summer of 1934 in boring fourteen holes around the Money Pit and reported these results to Blair:

No. 1 to the depth of 170 ft.:	At 58 ft. seam of pink sand (which Blair believed to be possibly the result of the red dye put down in 1899) From 132 to 146 feet, mud mixed with clay and gravel
No. 2 6 feet 11 inches from Chappell shaft: No. 8 14 feet from Chappell shaft: Nos. 13 and 14 to 136 feet:	At 58 feet seam of pink sand Below 110 feet bits of old oak Below 123 feet bits of old china Struck what was deemed to be a bulkhead made of oak and cement 14 inches thick. Drill dropped 33 feet to 169 feet and then entered bits of decayed oak to 176 feet where it struck solid matter

Nixon's agreement with Blair lapsed in November 1934 and he returned home like his predecessors, to count his losses. Blair was not unduly disturbed as another determined treasure seeker stood on the threshold, awaiting his permission to start work on the island.

11 Gilbert Hedden Excavates: Edwin Hamilton Explores

Frederick Blair at last found the rich and experienced engineer who might overcome the difficulties of recovering the treasure. This man, Gilbert D. Hedden, the Vice-President and General Manager of the Hedden Iron Construction Company of Hillside, New Jersey, had recently sold his business. His operations on the island were delayed until 1936 while Blair straightened out difficulties about the property. It was purchased from the heirs of Henry Sellers for $5,000 on 25 July 1935 and ownership was vested in a trustee acting for Hedden.

Hedden planned to drain and clean out the Money Pit. He contracted with Sprague and Henwood, who had worked previously on Oak Island, and put an experienced engineer named Frederick R. Krupp in charge of the work. He was assisted by Sylvester Carroll, a veteran Canadian gold miner. A 7,500 watt electric power line was run to the island from the mainland and turbine pumps, capable of sucki· up 1,000 gallons of water a minute, were installed in the Money Pit.

Work began in the Chappell shaft No. 21. Before the end of June a depth of 110 ft. was reached and then drills were employed to probe the area beneath. They brought up bits of oak from 150 ft. and encountered at 168 ft. large blocks of granite which had to be broken up before they could be lifted out. Below that depth the drills reached what appeared to be solid rock, probably shale or sandstone. The shaft was then excavated and cribbed down to 170 ft., the greatest depth so far reached. Nothing was found to confirm the presence of treasure in the adjacent Money Pit, either at that depth or farther down. That ended the season's work.

When operations were resumed in May of the following year, it was decided to sink a new shaft (No. 22) north-eastwards and close to the presumed site of the Money Pit.

This became known as the 'Hedden' shaft. The outlines of an old shaft, six ft. by ten ft., cribbed and in a good state of preservation, were found ten ft. down. This shaft included part of a previously excavated shaft which was believed to be the Money Pit itself. Uncertainty about its exact site remained. Old drill casings were found at fifty ft., and at sixty-five ft. an old miner's whale-oil lamp, at eighty ft. an ancient oak stump, and at ninety-three ft. an old collapsed tunnel and a band of clay 'resembling putty'. At 104 ft. the workmen came across a tunnel three ft. ten in. wide and six ft. four in. high, lined by six in. hemlock and oaken timber. Blair believed that this tunnel was part of one made about 1866, at the time when operators were certainly working within the original shaft.

Excavation of shaft No. 22 was stopped at 124½ ft. and fifteen holes were bored to a depth of forty-two ft. The drills bored through hard sand for twenty-three ft., and in five bores, between 148 and 157 ft. encountered oak varying from one in. to two ft. six in. in thickness. This appeared to be a new find.

Hedden's operations at the site ended with these inconclusive results. Though disappointed, Hedden nonetheless expressed his firm conviction that a number of treasure chests lay at the depth of 160 to 170 ft. They were encrusted in hard clay, and lay in soil that had been disturbed by a century and a half of haphazard digging. These chests, he thought, had doubtless rotted away, due to the vast amount of water present in the Money Pit. Much of the treasure might have become scattered and embedded in the belt of blue clay. He was convinced that the treasure must have been of enormous value to warrant the precautions taken to safeguard it.

Hedden totally rejected the popular conception of the existence of an iron and cement chamber in the depths of the Money Pit. The idea was too fantastic; men who possessed the engineering skill to harness the tides would not have placed their hoard below the level of the flood gates, which Heddon and others were convinced existed somewhere on the island. Equally fantastic, in his opinion, was the theory that chests had been placed at 98 ft. to distract attention from the real treasure which lay farther down. He also dismissed the belief in artificial cement; it was nothing more exciting than hardened clay with which the chests had become thoroughly encrusted.

Hedden camped on the island with Blair, giving him the opportunity to examine it thoroughly – something no previous operator had troubled to do. He noticed the enormous erosion its shores had suffered. At Smith's Cove he found the ends of two timbers projecting from the sand at low tide. The removal of four ft. of sand disclosed these ancient timbers to be about four ft. apart, fifteen in. in diameter and notched at every four ft. In each notch a heavy wooden pin had been inserted and in one notch, a cross piece four ft. long. These timbers were believed to have formed an ancient skidway, built at a period when wood was easier to work than iron, hence the wooden pins.

Whether or not Hedden had found a relic of the work of the original depositors, his curiosity led to a strange but mystifying discovery. Although he did not fully understand its significance, he had found the key to the mystery. I will explain this in due course (see Chapter 14).

After 140 years of backbreaking toil and vast expenditure the operators had achieved nothing and had learned nothing. The treasure, if it existed, was as safe from recovery as it had ever been. Convinced they needed only to conquer the flooding to reach it, the adventurers bailed and pumped, bored and dug, searching in between times for the mythical water gates somewhere below ground. They did not stop to consider how such a flood-locking system could have been devised, or could have withstood the deterioration of time. The adventurers had no time to think; they were in too much of a hurry. They all faced the same predicament; they must succeed quickly before their money ran out. They resolutely ignored the awful possibility that those who had concealed the treasure had returned to recover it.

An operator of a very different calibre now made his appearance. He carefully and methodically worked on the island for six years, but retired when he was beaten, not by the flooding, but by the Canadian 'call up' for the Second World War, which reduced his labour force from fourteen to two men.

I talked with Edwin H. Hamilton in 1966, twenty years after his retirement from the Money Pit venture and the professorship of mechanical engineering he held at New York University. He settled at Chester after the war where he owns a yacht-building yard. I found him there. 'I have only five minutes to spare', he told me pointing to a yacht his men were busy painting. 'It has to be in the water tonight by the time the owner arrives from New York.' We were still talking an hour later, and he spent five hours with me that evening telling me of his experiences on Oak Island.

Leasing the machinery that Hedden had left on the island, Hamilton started work near the Money Pit in July 1938, and bored fifty-eight holes to the depth of 168 to 171 ft. All reached solid limestone. In the fifteenth hole he struck iron at 157 ft. He cleared out shaft No. 21 which had been sunk in 1931 by William Chappell by digging and re-timbered it down to 170 ft. In his explorations between 1940 and 1943, Hamilton re-located an old Halifax tunnel leading into the Money Pit south-east of and close to the Hedden shaft (No. 22). From these discoveries, Hamilton concluded that the Chappell shaft (No. 21) was not located on the exact site of the original Money Pit but lay about five ft. south of it. In 1942, he sunk a shaft, measuring eight ft. square, to the depth of 168 ft. in the southern half of the Hedden shaft. It was about eight ft. from the Chappell shaft which also went to that depth. The two shafts were connected by an old tunnel, which had been driven by William Chappell. Hamilton drilled sideways and downwards from it in all directions, keeping the water down by the use of Hedden's powerful pumps.

Hamilton told me that this vertical and lateral drilling to 180 ft. disclosed things that should not have been there, such as stones that were not native to that depth of soil. He reached a greater depth than anyone had done previously and re-located the original shaft. He made two remarkable discoveries, though he received credit for neither of them. Hamilton located the inlet of the second water course, the existence of which had been suspected since 1897. This entered the *eastern* side of the Money Pit at 150 ft., forty ft. below the higher tunnel which brought water from Smith's Cove. It was obvious that the two artificial water tunnels both came from Smith's Cove, the original constructors having driven two tunnels, one above the other. This lower tunnel was not the tunnel found by the Halifax Company in 1866-7, the discovery of which S. C. Fraser, their foreman, had described in a letter to A. S. Lowden in 1895. That tunnel entered the Money Pit just below the flood tunnel at the 111 ft. level.

Hamilton's discovery of this second man-made flood tunnel from Smith's Cove raised the question: 'How then did the red dye which had been put into the Money Pit in 1897 reach the *south* shore where it showed itself in the water at three distinct places?' Hamilton answered my question: at the depth of 180 ft. he encountered a flood of water eight by ten in. wide and running from north-east to south-west. Analysis of samples brought to the surface showed that it was of greater specific gravity than the sea-water around the island. The inference was clear: through the depths of the Money Pit ran an underground natural stream, perhaps even a small river. Hamilton may have intercepted only one branch. Full discussion of the inference of Hamilton's discovery needs to be left until the operations conducted in 1965 are dealt with, as by then, research had been made into the geological nature of Oak Island's sub-soil.

Hamilton also investigated the 'well-like' hole into which Mrs Sellers' oxen had fallen in 1878. It became called the 'Cave-In' shaft. It had been opened up by Blair in 1895, and explained as an air-vent, sunk to facilitate the construction of the flood tunnel. Hamilton's researches render this theory improbable, as I shall explain later.

Hamilton retired from the scene in 1943. Like his predecessors, he was convinced that a great treasure lay in the depths of the Money Pit.

12 Four Men Die

The years immediately following the end of the Second World War were marked by a lull in the operations due to the division of 'rights' between Gilbert Hedden and Frederick Blair; the former owning the soil and the latter the exclusive right of search under his treasure trove agreement with the government. It was not until 1950 that the situation was finally cleared up. John Whitney Lewis, a New York mining engineer, purchased the property from Hedden, and applied for a licence to search under the Treasure Trove Act of that year. His application was opposed successfully by Blair, and by Melbourne Chappell, the son of the deceased William Chappell. Lewis conveyed the property to a trust company to hold on behalf of Chappell.

Several wild schemes were presented for Blair's attention at this time. During his sixty years' devotion to the Money Pit, he had corresponded politely and painstakingly with genuine enthusiasts, cranks and visionaries. Several people had offered pirate charts. One, which will be referred to later, seems to have related to Oak Island and may have been genuine. Another chart, which I shall discuss in due course, appears to fulfil that condition. Both were found, possibly together, by people who kept the information to themselves, unaware of its possible significance. I attempted to trace the descendants of the first chart's finder, following them to Boston, Massachusetts, where the trail ran cold. Several of the charts offered to Blair were obvious forgeries, pictorial recapitulations of the known facts. It required little imagination and skill to draw the well-publicised features of the island's famous 'works', and to add what was thought to be significant details, such as sluice gates designed to halt the flow of water, and an iron and cemented treasure vault in the depths of the Money Pit, a sealed and watertight chamber protected by the tides of the ocean. The more ingenious fakers estimated its size and filled it with the appropriate number of golden bars, valued at millions of dollars, blithely ignoring the improbability that the men who had concealed them would have abandoned such immense wealth forever. Genuine pirate charts are as rare as are pirate treasure caches.

Blair does not seem to have accepted the prevalent and extravagant theories of the Money Pit's origin. But, as we shall learn, he became vastly excited by the disclosure of a surprising piece of evidence. It is not yet opportune to discuss the dramatic discovery of the phoney chart which, none the less, carried the vital clue to the secrets of the Money Pit.

One faked chart was described in 1934. It no longer existed but its one-time owner, W. J. Doyle of Cabri, Saskatchewan, informed Blair that he knew it was a map of Oak Island for 'it showed how the water got in and how to shut it off'. Doyle came to Nova Scotia where he showed Blair a plan marked 'Oak Island'. It showed 'a gate so rigged to act like a clapper, allowed the water to pass inward from the shore, but not outward', which could be closed by the pull of a chain. Blair placed no credence in Doyle's story. Whether or not he was the same man is unknown, but a man named Doyle wrote to Hedden in 1945, enclosing a tracing from an 'old pirate map'. This appeared to be no more than a reproduction of a map printed in 1935.

Blair placed no greater confidence in the 'gold finders', mediums and advocates of 'automatic writing' and photography who offered to help him. The correspondence kept by Blair shows that interest in the Money Pit was widespread. A young man turned up at Oak Island with a pick and shovel who had purchased for $125 a map sold at a radio auction in New York. He was followed by another man from New York, Edward Reichert, who came to Nova Scotia in 1946, but when he learned of the difficulties already encountered, he abandoned his plans. In the following year, a retired US army officer, Colonel H. A. Gardner, was granted leave to attempt 'to determine the exact location of the treasure' by radar; his equipment failed to work.

Frederick Blair died on 1 April 1951. The treasure trove rights passed to Melbourne Chappell who decided to work the site himself. Employing a radar device, he chose a spot north of the Money Pit, and with the aid of a clamshell digger, he excavated to the depth of forty-six ft. He encountered soft soil which indicated previous work at that spot, but we have no hint of the nature of that work. That ended

Chappell's operations.

Then a Texan oil drilling syndicate, led by George J. Greene of Corpus Christi, started operations in October 1955. Greene was quoted in the Corpus Christi *Caller*, 29 September, as saying that he proposed to cut off the water from the Money Pit by sinking steel casing ten ft. in diameter into the hole. If this did not cut off the water, it would at least allow divers to work below without the fear of the sides caving in. His syndicate, announced Greene, was prepared to spend money without limit to prove or disprove the legend of Oak Island. 'Water doesn't bother an oil man,' he asserted. The tough part was to find the treasure and if he could find it he would get it out. On the day he retired from the scene, Greene stated, '*someone* went to a lot of trouble to bury *something* here. And unless he was the greatest practical joker of all time, it must have been well worth the effort.'

During his four weeks on Oak Island, Greene drilled along a line on the north side of the Chappell shaft (No. 21). The first boring reached to 190 ft., striking various 'voids'. The fourth encountered oak timbers eight in. thick at a hundred ft., then a void, then a cavity of forty-five ft. and finally hard clay. Greene was quoted by the *Caller* on 28 October, by which time he had returned home, as saying, 'We poured 100,000 gallons of water into it and it ran out, but where I don't know.'

The discovery of this extensive cavity, which seems to have been re-located in 1965, was accepted as confirmation of the existence of the sealed water-tight chamber at the bottom of the Money Pit for which so many explorers had been searching. No one considered this void might be no more than a natural cavern, as is found often in limestone formations.

In 1961, Brian Backmann, a public relations consultant who lived at Chester, brought a team of skin divers. They searched around the island for traces of ships which might have anchored there. Close to the south shore they found traces of what appeared to be the foundations of a coffer-dam which Backmann believes was used to hold back the sea while the original depositors constructed an entrance into the Money Pit. They intended, on their return, to rebuild the coffer-dam.

About this time, the early 1960s, the local surveyor, F. C.

Nolan, who owned property across the neck of the island, made a survey of the eastern part of the island. He put down a line of bench marks.

Two other men became interested in the island. They had no connection with one another but a division of the treasure trove rights enabled them to work independently. Robert E. Restall, a fifty-six-year-old former circus stunt rider from Hamilton, Ontario, concerned himself principally with the Money Pit. W. L. Johnson, from Vancouver, concentrated his attention elsewhere.

Johnson came to the island to think rather than to dig. He was the first to use brains rather than brawn and worked out a theory. In 1962 he drilled holes and made a small excavation some distance from the Money Pit.

Restall was reputed to be backed by twenty friends who put up $100,000 between them. He stated, 'I am on the trail of great wealth.' He took up residence at the site with his English-born wife, Mildred, and their four sons. 'The gold bars are within my grasp,' declared Restall as he started to re-excavate the Money Pit. He was convinced the treasure he was seeking lay in its depths. 'Anyone can reach the gold who has enough backing and the proper equipment,' he confidently predicted.

Restall worked on the island for five years. On 17 August 1963 he, his son John, aged twenty-two, and two other treasure seekers, Cyril Hiltz, aged twenty-two and Carl Graeser, aged forty, were killed in an underground tunnel beneath the shaft they had dug close to Smith's Cove. Peter Beamish from Andover, Massachusetts, who was camping on the island with a party of students, told me how the accident happened: the day was hot and humid; the exhaust fumes from the pump working at the top of the shaft sank into its depths; Restall climbed down, slipped and fell. He became affected by the carbon monoxide gas; his son jumped in to rescue him. He too became unconscious. Hiltz and Graeser followed, as did four other would-be rescuers. Within a short time eight men had entered the shaft. All became affected by the gas to some degree. Beamish and the students, using ropes, brought them up; four recovered and four died. Counting the unknown man who had been scalded to death when the pumping engine burst in 1860, the Money Pit had now claimed five victims.

Before his death, Restall had found a stone inscribed with

the date '1704'. This led him to conclude that the treasure had been buried in that year.

In June 1965, Oak Island was visited by John Gwynne-Evans from London. He investigated the island's geological structure and commissioned an aerial survey. With the aid of Colin Summers from Worthing, England, he drew a plan showing the principal landmarks. Summers transferred it to a transparency corresponding to the aerial photograph. Their survey is a useful guide to the location of some of these landmarks. They were removed later that year.

The American petroleum geologist, Robert Dunfield, came to the island before Restall's death. Excited, as a boy, by the story of the long treasure hunt, Dunfield had never forgotten it. Now, aged thirty-nine, he took over Restall's concession and he commenced work on 1 September 1965. I corresponded and spoke with Dunfield who permitted me, in his absence, to inspect the island in June 1966. By that time much of its eastern end had been wrecked.

Dunfield was, I understand, supported by twenty-four partners. He set out to excavate deeper than anyone had before him. He built a causeway from the mainland along which to bring the 70 ft.-high clam-digger he had hired to the site. He set to work to re-excavate the Money Pit. On 2 November he was reported in the Halifax *Herald Chronicle* as saying: 'We thought at first it would take only three weeks, but we make discoveries every day that make us change our opinions. I can't predict how long we will be here.' By 22 December, he had excavated a shaft eighty ft. wide and 130 ft. deep. The winter rains came and the shaft caved in. 'We've got a tiger by the tail and we are not going to let go,' Dunfield stated, adding 'We will finish this thing one way or the other.'

During his drilling operations Dunfield re-located, apparently, the large cavity at the 140 ft. level which had been found by Greene in 1955. His drill broke through its roof, dropped for forty ft., and brought up a concrete-like material of which Dunfield sent specimens to Montreal for analysis. It was identified as gypsum, a whitish material which may have been the substance previously identified as cement. Whether or not this is the correct interpretation, Dunfield believed (*Herald Chronicle*, 15 March 1966) that his drilling had disclosed, from 139 to 184 ft. down, a chamber roofed with wood and floored with iron. He was confident that there 'is something deep beneath the island's surface, if it is only some weird rock formation'. On the question of whether or not this was due to the Windsor Rock Formation, a fault of which is believed to run beneath Oak Island, Dunfield was non-committal.

While Dunfield worked at the Money Pit, one of his partners supervised another team of workmen. They excavated an elongated crater, fifty ft. long and twenty ft. wide, at the site of the stone triangle (noticed first in 1897 and rediscovered in 1937), which they removed or covered. This operation was intended to locate and intercept the water course to the Money Pit which was believed to run from the southern shore of the island. It disclosed a shaft beneath the base of the triangle which appeared to be part of the original work but this massive excavation failed to stop the flooding. Dunfield turned his attention to Smith's Cove. He dug a deep trench parallel to the beach and he excavated a crater, eighty ft. wide and a hundred ft. deep, at the site of the cave-in shaft, the 'bell-like' hole into which Mrs Sellers' oxen had fallen. It disappeared completely into the depths.

'If we can't make it this time, we will leave it to someone else', stated Dunfield on 10 February. A month later he remarked, 'I'm running out of nerve but I'm damned if I'll quit. I'm going on till I succeed or bust, and I intend to succeed.' On 15 March he stated that his six months' work had cost $120,000 and 'my nerves show it. There's a limit to everything and I've gone about as far as I can go.' Seven days later, he called a temporary halt, returning to California 'until the weather gets better'. In a final press interview, Dunfield stated he would return to finish the job. He did not think that the Money Pit was a 'lost cause'. He knew where the water that flooded the Money Pit came from; he had excluded every area of the island except Smith's Cove.

In a letter written to the Halifax *Herald Chronicle*, which quoted from it on 12 May 1966, Dunfield stated that he expected to return shortly when 'the mystery will be resolved one way or another'. He would excavate one more hole. Speaking by telephone from his home in Canoga Park, California, on 1 July, Dunfield said that his men were preparing the machines to 're-dig the prospect hole'.

When I visited the island again in 1967, its eastern end

had been devastated: the stone triangle and the two drilled rocks [the discovery and significance of which I shall consider later] had disappeared; the cave-in shaft had become a water-filled crater, eighty ft. wide; the Money Pit itself had become refilled with earth to within ten ft. of the surface; within this eighty ft. wide depression rose the timbered shaft, which had been constructed by Hedden.

I wandered over the island and through the spruce woods which now cover all but the area cleared around the Money Pit, and down to Smith's Cove. At the south-eastern point of the island lay the last two ancient and once umbrella-shaped oaks, which had formerly covered the whole island, giving it its now famous name. Two only remained, they were both dead and had toppled amongst the spruce trees. The last oaks had gone from Oak Island; according to local legend when that happened the island would give up its secret.

Dunfield's concession was taken over in 1967 by a group from Montreal. Its twelve members, who included Dunfield and Restall's widow, obtained the search rights from M. R. Chappell, the owner of the island's eastern end.

This group is headed by David Tobias with whom I talked in Montreal in 1967. In 1970 it became incorporated as the Triton Alliance Company, which, according to the Montreal *Financial Post* on 21 March, intended to spend as much as $520,000. Tobias and his associates (of whom M. R. Chappell, Daniel Blakenship and Donald C. Webster were named) were stated to be confident that Triton could get to the bottom of the mystery. Their reason: 'we are the first people to know what to expect and what we are after'. The Alliance had been encouraged by the results of previous drilling parties sponsored by Tobias: 'It located wide areas of bedrock 165 feet down and a peculiar depression where the bedrock was not reached until 200 feet plus. The drill went through the 165 feet levels of bedrock around this depression.

'Four cavities were found beneath the bedrock, at levels deeper than 200 feet.'

The report continued:

Triton was formed following this drilling programme.

Triton's intention this summer is to follow up these finds with a new shaft, to be excavated by a specialist company on a fixed-cost contract. From the main shaft, the cavities and other areas of interest will be explored laterally.

Before the shaft is sunk, a final preparatory drilling programme will investigate the problems of flooding and determine costs for the shaft.

This programme starts next week. The shaft is expected to go down in April-May.

Tobias expects the entire Triton project to be completed before winter.

He believes the chances of striking it rich are four-to-one.

Tobias was quick to say that 'the dig will be the most expensive of its kind ever undertaken in Canada'.

He likes to refer to it as an archaeological and historical project, rather than a treasure hunt. Triton investors came forward without pressure, he says. They are interested in the project as a 'kind of hobby'. Tight money and stock-market gloom did not deter them.

Triton do not intend to excavate a large crater at the site of the Money Pit. Their work has been confined to the drilling of holes of sufficient diameter to permit searchers to examine conditions at considerable distances below the surface.

On 23 November 1971 (Halifax *Herald Chronicle*) Triton announced the discovery, by drilling, of a cavity at 212 ft., below bedrock. A submarine television camera had been lowered and the report stated:

A series of pictures show faint outlines of what project manager Dan Blakenship says he is certain are three chests, one having a handle on the end and a curved top. Besides another of the chests or boxes, he says, is some sort of tool, not unlike a pick-axe.

Another view clearly shows three logs lying on the floor of the chamber, more than 40 feet deeper than any previous treasure seekers had ever explored, Mr Blakenship said.

A more gruesome revelation by the camera probing the same cell was the appearance on the monitor of a human hand, partly clenched, suspended in water, Mr Blakenship said.

Startled by what he saw, Mr Blakenship said he summoned all his workers, one by one, into the shack housing the television monitor. Each man confirmed that the hand, still covered with flesh, had what looked like a slash mark across the back, while below the mark the mangled flesh suggested it had been torn or chopped from the wrist, he said.

Blakenship told the reporter that he had sought the advice of experts who told him that under certain conditions it would be possible for human flesh to be preserved, especially if it had been embedded in clay, such as is found at great depths on Oak Island. Drilling could have caused the hand to break loose in the water.

Triton have also uncovered, at Smith's Cove, ancient logs, 160 feet long, notched exactly every four feet and each marked with a Roman numeral. Laboratory tests on wood samples indicated that they were at least 250 years old.

The Triton Group believe that the island was used as a communal bank by pirates. A triangular-shaped stone found on the island is said to be identical to those found at entrances to pirates' communal banks in the Indies.

The published photograph is too indefinite for a fair assessment of Triton's discovery. Presumably, they will excavate to reach the cavity at 212 ft. Various indications suggest that it is north of the Money Pit and it is difficult to see any connection between it and the original shaft. The depths of Oak Island may be honeycombed with cavities, small solution caverns as are found in limestone formations. (See Postscript 1.)

13 I Visit Oak Island

The long search for treasure has proved costly and frustrating. Nothing has been found to prove its existence. The only evidence that those impregnable defences were designed to protect a concealment is circumstantial; it is difficult otherwise to account for them.

This is a treasure-hunt in reverse. Such ventures stem, usually, from a sailor's yarn, or by the discovery of a sea-stained chart. The Money Pit was found by chance. There is no strong tradition of such an undertaking. No one talked. The men who worked on the island left nothing behind to disclose their identity; not a buckle or button, shattered pick or broken spade. They must have cleaned up the ground. Yet, the Pit's designer seems to have expected and even invited discovery. He left the tell-tale oak tree standing, its lopped branch mute testimony that someone had used it as a hoist, and had dug below. It would have been easy to have uprooted the tree and let it fall across the shaft. Chance visitors would have concluded that it had blown down in a storm. The Money Pit might never have been found.

The work of digging and tunnelling, and the construction of the water-catchment, must have taken considerable time. A civil engineer, experienced in underground work, has given his opinion that, with the tools available, it would have required the exertions of at least one hundred men, working three shifts a day, for a minimum of six months.

Such work could have been done only by a disciplined and experienced force, and designed and carried out by an engineering genius. He conceived an extraordinary plan of concealment. He harnessed the tides of the ocean to protect his shaft. He believed that his defences were impregnable, knowing that attempts to defeat them could lead only to maddening frustration. He was no ordinary man. We need to call him 'Mr X'. Did he return to recover his cache? That fearful possibility has been cheerfully ignored by the host of treasure hunters: The smell of treasure trove has warped their judgment. They have tried to overwhelm the problem rather than solve it.

I prefer to tackle it as a mystery, a puzzle worth solving. My interest was aroused in 1939 by the article *The Money Pit*, contributed to the *Saturday Evening Post* by Parker Morrell who had visited the island and talked with Gilbert Hedden. The story of the long and fruitless search fascinated me; the Money Pit's impregnable defences intrigued my imagination. I cut out the article, little realizing how the story would affect my life. My interest revived in 1950 and I determined to learn more about Oak Island and its mystery.

I wrote to Melbourne Chappell, the owner of the island. He referred me to Gordon Blair who loaned me his father's records, telling me the history of the operations and the beliefs of the early searchers in greater detail. I did not know enough to question their basic assumption: that an immense treasure lay at the depths of the Money Pit. That seemed obvious; why else had its impregnable defences been required? I accepted that its recovery necessitated huge expenditure and considerable engineering skill, neither of which I possessed.

I concentrated on the men who had dug the Pit. How had they planned to recover their treasure from its flooded depths? I heard the theory that they had provided an easy 'walk-in' tunnel, its entrance some distance from the Pit, by which to reach the sealed and water-tight chamber which was believed to exist between 150 and 170 ft.

I became obsessed with the problem which, lacking technical knowledge, I felt ill-equipped to solve. I looked for a surveyor who, like myself, might become an enthusiastic 'addict' and was fortunate to find Roy Lewis Reynish, FRIBA, who lived nearby at Chichester, Sussex. We examined the Roper Survey, made in 1937, a copy of which I had obtained from Nova Scotia. It provided the physical facts. I sought further information.

My visit to the Map Room of the British Museum proved useful. I had been preceded, I learned, by the Londoner John Gwynne-Evans, who was at that moment in Nova Scotia. On a subsequent visit, the Superintendent of the Map Room drew my attention to his correspondence in 1960 with the American investigator, Alarik Walton, who had sent several drawings of the island's works with a Note. (I had failed to find it on my earlier visit due to the Map

Room file being identified as 'Smith's Island', the name given to Oak Island by Charles Morris in 1762.) The correspondence had ceased as abruptly as it had begun. My letter to Walton's address at San Diego, California, was returned with the note, 'Gone away'. I contacted him finally in 1971. He has asked me not to discuss the ideas he publicized in 1960, and for which he now claims priority. I respect his wishes, although, in my opinion, he did not then establish anything remarkable. He was on the right track, no more. Possibly he has since expanded his ideas to form a definite theory, about which he is reticent.

Gwynne-Evans, whom I met on his return to London, told me about his visit to the island, and his encounters with two other investigators, Colin Summers of Worthing, Sussex, and W. L. Johnson of Vancouver, British Columbia. Summers gave me a copy of the survey, linked to an air-photograph, which he and Gwynne-Evans had made. He also told me he had discovered that the 'road', observed in 1795, disappeared and ran beneath the swamp on the southern shore. Its continuation on the other side would have brought it directly to the stone triangle which was found in 1937. This suggests that the road had been constructed before the swamp encroached, possibly before 1785, when the road was employed as a boundary between lots. I have corresponded with Johnson since 1966. He has given me unstinted help, disclosing his own theories, and his reasoning.

I now knew far more about the 'facts', and the many theories that had been advanced. One thing remained to be done. I flew to Nova Scotia in June 1966, and I went again in the following year.

Following my visits to the site, Reynish and I set out my information in the form of a Plan, illustrating the island's works. It occupied us for two years. We followed many false scents and winding trails, clue after clue crumbled into dust; realization of the truth came slowly.

I believe that I have largely solved the mystery. I qualify that statement because certain facts remain obscure. That is not surprising since work on the island was a clandestine operation and 'Mr X' did not intend that we should penetrate his secrets.

These had, however, been partly revealed in 1937, due to Gilbert Hedden's curiosity about the people who had dug the Money Pit.

14 A Mysterious Map

Hedden had a mystifying experience. He came across a book, published in England in 1935 and entitled *Captain Kidd and His Skeleton Island*. Its author, Harold Tom Wilkins, included a crude drawing of an island on which was placed a set of directions.

Comparison of this map with Oak Island indicated fourteen marked resemblances: the general outline of the two islands was similar; the 'Lagoon' shown on the map corresponded to the indentation on Oak Island's south-western shore, the points of which appeared to have once been joined by a ridge of gravel. (This is discernible still in some aerial photographs.) The lagoon ended its career as the swamp, triangular in shape, which eats into the shore. The shoals, depths and reefs, depicted in the map, corresponded with those features around the island; its elevations were similar to those shown on the map; traces of ancient ponds were identical with those illustrated. The best anchorage on the island, at Smith's Cove, was shown, and a cross marked a spot which seemed to correspond with the location of the Money Pit. The compass directions given on the map, which was dated 1669, approximated to those that applied to Oak Island.

These similarities (some of which appear to have existed only in Hedden's imagination), suggested that the published map might depict Oak Island. Hedden scanned the set of directions which called for the laying out of a course. They were as follows:

18 W and by 7 E on Rock
30 S W   14 N Tree
7 by 8 by 4.

Carrying the book, its pages open at the map, Hedden searched the area around the Money Pit. Fifty ft. to its north he found a large granite stone, three ft. in length, in which a hole two in. deep and one and a quarter in. in diameter had

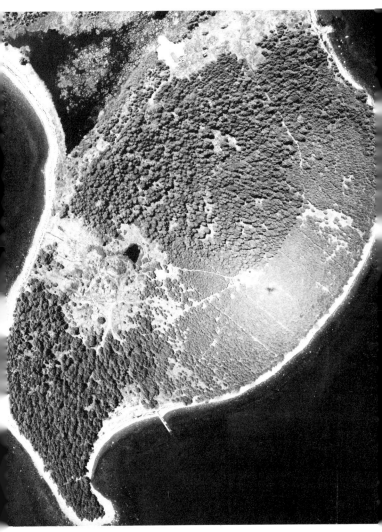

4. Close-up aerial view of the Money Pit area, taken in 1965. This photograph registers the positions of the Money Pit, the two Drilled Rocks and the Stone Triangle, before they were obliterated or removed in 1965/6. (Scale 148ft to 1 inch. Altitude 1,800 ft).

5. Oak Island. Air photograph taken from south-east. 1972.

6. Survey made in 1785 by William Nelson, with names of grantees of land added up to 1818. The line between the plots represents the road first noticed in 1795.

7. The Money Pit in 1955, during Charles Greene's operations.

been drilled. He ran to tell Blair about his discovery and was greeted with the exclamation, 'there is another stone marked in exactly the same way near the beach at Smith's Cove'. He and his partners, said Blair, had noticed it forty years before and wondered what it might mean. Blair relocated this boulder which was embedded in sand and he and Hedden stepped out the distance between the two drilled rocks. It measured approximately twenty-five rods, the sum of eighteen and seven (see directions above), indicating that rods had been the unit of measure employed, if these marker stones had any meaning.

Hedden called in the Provincial Land Surveyor, Charles Roper who came to Oak Island on 16 August 1937 with his assistant, George Bates. Roper and Bates told me in 1966 that they were not informed of Hedden's reasons for the survey. They said the two drilled rocks were encrusted with moss and looked as though they had been in the same position for centuries. They lay on a line south of west, parallel to the supposed line of the subterranean flood tunnel from Smith's Cove to the Money Pit.

These two drilled rocks, Roper and Bates found, lay 421½ ft. apart, nine ft. in excess of the exact equivalent of twenty-five rods, which is 312 ft. Nevertheless, they measured a position seven rods from the rock near Smith's Cove and eighteen rods from the rock by the Money Pit. Then, following the directions, they turned south-west, measuring out the distance of thirty rods, or 495 ft., bringing the surveyors to a dense tangle of bushes close to high water mark on the southern shore. A man employed by Hedden, named Amos Nanse, crawled in. His excited cry brought the searchers. They found Nanse pointing to a set of beach stones embedded in the soil. Clearing away the bushes, Hedden and his men discovered the stone triangle that had been noticed by Captain Welling in 1897.

Each side of the triangle was ten ft. long. A half circle of stones enclosed its base giving the whole structure the appearance of a sextant. An arrow of stones fourteen ft. long connected this curved base with the triangle's apex.

Setting up his transit and sighting it along the line of the arrow shaft, Roper peered through his view-finder. 'North,' he announced, quickly qualifying his finding by the statement that the direction was True and not Magnetic North. 'It points,' he exclaimed. 'Come, and look for yourselves,' he invited. Hedden peered through the viewfinder. The arrow pointed directly towards the Money Pit.

The directions, concluded Hedden, led to the Money Pit. No one could fathom the meaning of the cryptic numbers '7 By 8 By 4'.

The relevance of the directions to Oak Island was enough for Blair. 'This settles it,' he told Hedden, 'Kidd must have planted the treasure. We will go to England to get to the bottom of this.' Hedden travelled to London in 1938 where he traced the author of the book about Kidd. Harold Wilkins

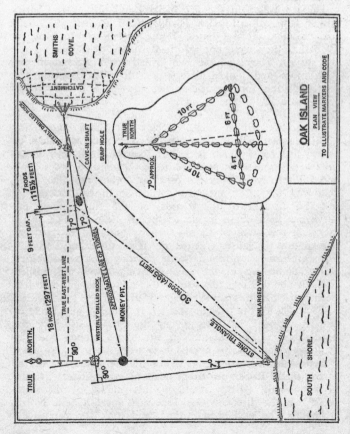

OAK ISLAND

PLAN VIEW

TO ILLUSTRATE MARKERS AND CODE

was dumbfounded when he was told of the similarities between his map and Oak Island. He stated emphatically that his map could have no possible connection with an island in Nova Scotia; it was a composite map of an island in the China Sea which he had drawn from memory. He had been allowed to see four ancient charts which had been found in three sea chests and a desk which had undoubtedly once belonged to Captain Kidd. Their owner, Hubert Palmer of Eastbourne, Sussex, had not allowed him to inspect either the latitude or longitude given or the directions with which two of the charts were inscribed.

When asked where he had derived the set of directions from with which he had embellished his map, Wilkins said at first that he could not remember. He might have noted them from one of the thousands of charts and manuscripts he had inspected during the researches into his several books about pirates and treasure troves. Wilkins was willing to concede that his directions fitted Oak Island, but he could not help Hedden further. He said more, as Hedden subsequently described in a letter to Blair:

> He almost immediately admitted that the chart as shown in the Kidd book is simply a figment of his imagination and apologised sincerely for not being able to tell me what it was. I am sure he is getting into a bit of hot water in that regard as he has received many letters from all over the world in which the writer professes to identify the island and offers to give its location. He admitted my claims to identify far surpassed any others he had received and agreed that his drawing was according to the evidence undoubtedly of Oak Island. When he had submitted his book to the publishers they demanded that he included some sort of map or chart. He put the request up to Palmer who absolutely refused to permit any of the charts (i.e. those he had found in the Kidd relics) to be reproduced. Wilkins therefore drew the chart as shown using symbols and marks shown on contemporary charts on file at the British Museum. The only actual marks included were the valley and the lagoon and he unconsciously made the general shape somewhat the same as the actual Kidd chart. The legend of the directing measurements simply came out of his mind and had no basis of fact at all. Later, just before the book was published, it was necessary to make a frontispiece, and not having the first drawing in his possession at that time, Wilkins reproduced it as well as he could from memory which accounts for the difference between the chart in the book and the one on

99

the front and last page. After I had convinced him that I had actually found markers at the points designated in his imaginary directions, he was amazed and went to great lengths to convince me that he had never been in America and had never seen an outline of Oak Island.

As Wilkins became more and more convinced of the truth of Hedden's story, he 'began to be convinced that he was a reincarnation of Kidd or some other pirate and had been selected to disclose the secrets of this long hidden hoard to the modern world. By the time I left he was completely certain of it, and will no doubt very shortly write a book on that theme.' Hedden thought that a good commentary on Wilkins's character and mental capacity. Wilkins died in 1958.

Hedden obtained a meeting with Hubert Palmer who confirmed that the Kidd charts represented an island in the China Sea. He assured Hedden that they did not bear the directions which he sought.

Hedden returned to America believing that somewhere in England there existed an original chart or note made by the man who had concealed treasure on Oak Island. The thought that a clue to the recovery of the treasure might exist was tantalizing and maddening.

Wilkins did not tell Hedden the truth. How I learned the source of the directions he had printed is a complicated story, typical of treasure-trove investigation. Important information falls into the hands of secretive, suspicious people who keep it to themselves for fear of being exploited. It is of no use by itself; they do not know how it could fit into the jig-saw someone else is trying to put together. Wilkins was obsessed by the fear that other people were out to steal his secrets. The man from whom he obtained the directions, which fitted the markers on Oak Island, believed that he had been guided by ghostly pirates, whose spirits would haunt him, should he divulge their secrets. The 'third man', he who eventually unravelled the mystery for me, shares some of these feelings.

I met Robert Gay on my second visit to Halifax. He is obsessed by his search for Captain Kidd's treasure, believing it is hidden in Nova Scotia, but not on Oak Island. I showed him copies of the Kidd-Palmer charts, which he had not seen, but he dismissed them as fakes, possibly because they did not conform to his clues. He was reluctant to discuss matters of mutual interest. I learned why later. He believed that I had been planted as a 'spy' to trap him into admissions which would show he had abused the confidence of his informant. Several months elapsed before, in correspondence, Gay told me about Herman Westhaver.

Westhaver died at Englishtown, Cape Breton Island, in March 1967. He had been a pilot, working in St Margaret's Bay, the next bay to Mahone Bay. In 1912 he and another pilot, Amos Smith, found a box containing charts in a cairn of stones on Cockrane's or Redmond's Island in Shad Bay, fifteen miles to the north of Mahone Bay. According to Westhaver, they were led there by a 'ghostly-pirate ship', and guided by an apparition. More probably they stumbled upon the cairn of stones by chance. What exactly they found in the box is uncertain.

In 1930 Frederick Blair heard of a chart possessed by Amos Smith. Later, his correspondent, Amos's grandson, James, made a Statutory Declaration at Roxbury, Massachusetts, where he lived:

> When I was a boy living at home in Greenfield, County of Colchester, Nova Scotia, I frequently heard my father, John J. Smith, speak of a chart, then in the possession of his father, Amos Smith, who lived in Shaw's Cove (Shad Bay) County of Halifax, Nova Scotia.
> According to my father, John J. Smith, the chart had reference to the burial of a quantity of gold on an island in Chester Basin, Nova Scotia, and that my grandfather Amos Smith, who had been a pilot working in and out of Halifax Harbour, claimed that the longitude and latitude given in the said chart was in the vicinity of the entrance to Chester Basin, and that the island was Oak Island.
> I heard so much talk about this chart that when I became older, I determined to see and examine it personally, and to that end I went to the house of my grandfather Amos Smith, where I saw and examined it, and read and studied its contents most carefully.
> According to the best of my recollection and belief, the chart told of the burial of a quantity of gold on an island located near this longitude and latitude, the figures of which I do not now remember. The chart showed that the island was about one mile in length, and about one half mile in width, shaped like a bottle, two coves at the north and east end, forming the bottleneck; and the island was wooded with oak trees. The chart stated that on a hill between the two coves, on the north or north-east end, a pit was dug to a

101

depth of 165 feet, near a large oak tree, from a limb of which they hung a block and tackle, and that a vault was constructed at the bottom of the pit, and the vault was walled with granite stone eighteen-inches thick, and that the inside was lined with two-ply of lead one-half-inch thick. The vault was filled with gold bars, each four feet long and four inches square and it was then covered with granite slabs. Two tunnels were dug forty-five feet below sea-level, at low tide, leading from the pit to the shore, in opposite directions, and there was placed in each tunnel an iron gate arranged so as to stop the flow of water, but these gates were left open to permit the water to flow through.

The chart was inadvertently destroyed with other old papers, the property of Amos Smith, after his decease.

Clearly, John Smith had heard the well-publicized story of the long search for treasure on Oak Island and his statement establishes no more than that his grandfather's chart may have referred to that island. It is now impossible to learn whether this chart was destroyed. It may have already passed into Westhaver's possession, or he and Amos may have acquired different charts from the same source.

Mutual interest in Kidd brought Gay and Westhaver together. Westhaver liked to play games with his friends, to tantalize them with half-truths, inviting them to guess the rest, and binding them by oaths of secrecy and 'death-bed' promises. He showed Gay a chart he had found in 1912, drawn on thick paper and in a very dilapidated condition. After his death, Westhaver promised, it would come to Gay with other information. One batch of papers reached Gay in 1967. The rest, including the chart, would be given to him on the '8th' day of an '8th' month, in a year which included the numeral '8'. On 8 August 1968, the likely date, Gay was in hospital and missed the appointed rendez-vous.

Gay does not know the identity of the man who holds the chart. Fortunately he had made a contemporaneous sketch after Westhaver had shown it to him. Neither he nor Westhaver had been able to identify the island depicted. Gay sought my advice.

He drew the island in outline. Soundings and lines indicating latitude and longitude were marked. Two named ships and an 'anchor' were depicted off the island's shores, beyond the island's south-western shore. The interior of the island bore two 'marks'. The chart was dated '17-8', and carried the directions which Wilkins had printed. The inward sailing course was indicated by an arrow and by the directions '40 N × 63 W Steer N.W. 3/4'. The chart also bore the mysterious letters, 'H.S.O.H.E.' It was named, in the old style of lettering, '*Gloucefter Ifle*'.

The name left me in no doubt of the island's identity. The British Admiralty Hydrographer, Joseph Frederick Wallet Des Barres, surveyed Mahone Bay in 1773. He named the bay, '*Mecklenburg Bay*' and Oak Island, '*Gloucefter Ifle*'. He called many of the islands after members of the Royal Family. The inference was clear. The man who had drawn the chart which Westhaver had found had based his drawing on the Des Barres chart. The island's name was inscribed close to the shore in exactly the place where Des Barres had positioned it. The anchor, and the soundings, were depicted with similar accuracy. These remarkable similarities suggest that the man had cut from a copy of Des Barres's chart the section surrounding the island. He used it to record the directions that fitted the island's markers.

Wilkins's possession of these directions is explained by his correspondence with Westhaver, which Gay has kept. Westhaver consulted Wilkins in order to learn the island's identity. They got into touch, probably through a mutual friend, James Patrick Nolan, whose treasure-hunting career Wilkins subsequently recorded (*A Modern Treasure Hunter*, 1948).

The man who employed a copy of Des Barres's chart could not have done so until after it had been printed. Between 1763 and 1773 Des Barres was engaged in surveying the coasts of Nova Scotia. Though trained as an engineer at the Royal Military College, Woolwich, he was commissioned by Admiral Howe to prepare these, and other charts of the Atlantic coast, for publication. He went to London in 1774 to supervise their printing, between 1779 and 1782, in the four volumes of his *Atlantic Neptune*. When the war with the American colonists broke out in 1775 these charts were urgently required. Certain of them were printed separately. Jealously guarded in wartime, these unique charts would have been available only to naval and military officers.

Henry Stevens, Son and Stiles, the publishers of *Notes Biographical and Bibliographical on the Atlantic Neptune*, London, 1937, inform me that the first issue of the chart of Mecklenburg Bay (as Des Barres named Mahone Bay), is dated 17 May 1776. The Stevens collection of Des Barres's charts consists of 176 folios containing 111 main charts, thirty-nine sheets of views and variants amounting to 807 items. In 1969 the National Maritime Museum completed a catalogue of these charts and the Librarian informed me that there are eight variants of chart No. 28 (*Atlantic Neptune*, Vol. I) that of Mecklenburg Bay. The year when Des Barres drew the chart is established by the magnetic variation: he noted the value as '13.30W', which operated in 1773.

Des Barres's name of *Gloucester Isle* for Oak Island was not generally adopted and was known probably only within official circles.

The chart found by Westhaver could not have been drawn before 1776. The implications of that being the earliest date for the recording of the directions, which fit the markers on Oak Island, and which Wilkins so fortunately printed, need to await later discussion.

When I informed Gay of my identification of the charted island, he lost interest in the matter. Like Westhaver, he thought that the chart might provide a further clue to Kidd's treasure.

Unreliable as the information derived from Wilkins and Westhaver may be, it is reasonable to conclude that Westhaver found the chart on Cockrane's or Redmond's island, Shad Bay. How it got there in the first place is a mystery. It could, perhaps, have been the chart brought to Nova Scotia between 1870 and 1880 by the mysterious visitor who called himself 'Captain Allen'. He came to Chester, the town on the northern shore of Mahone Bay, apparently from the Southern States, and 'had plenty of money, was of handsome appearance and well dressed, and wore a large white broad-brimmed hat'. He is also described as 'dark complexioned and talking with a foreign accent'. He purchased a small sloop from a fisherman in Shad Bay, who has been identified as a man named Ganter.

Allen had an ancient chart believed to be worded in a foreign language which he examined frequently but kept to himself. Early every morning he sailed from the bay and made for a position thirty miles off shore, which has been identified as 44° N. and 63° W. There he took the altitude of the sun. He then sailed shorewards on a compass bearing, apparently to the north-west, checking his course on his chart which he spread about on the deck of the vessel and would not permit his crew to examine. He kept this up day after day for two whole summers. He then disappeared and was never seen again.

According to local reports Oak Island was the only place he could have struck on that course. But he never landed there. After Allen's (if that was his true name), disappearance, a man from Halifax named Pickles, took over the sloop and adopted the same tactics. He said that Allen had given him certain compass directions, the latitude and longitude of his starting point, and had told him that he was searching for an island on which there was 'a huge cache of treasure, so huge that it was beyond imagination'. He explained that he was a rich man and did not care about the treasure, but thought that its recovery would be for the benefit of mankind. Pickles had no more success than Allen. He is said to have disclosed certain information about the island for which he was searching. He was directed by a fisherman named Billy Bull to Redmond's Island in Shad Bay and is reported to have found there the three piles of stones he was looking for, but not the well shown on the mysterious chart.

Allen may have been looking for Oak Island. Perhaps he missed Mahone Bay and sailed into St Margaret's Bay because he failed to reconcile the magnetic variation of the compass at his time with the value in the year in which the chart was drawn. A six or seven degree turn to the west would have taken him into Mahone Bay. He may have been confused. His chart may also have been based on Des Barres's survey. If so, it would have named Mahone Bay as 'Mecklenburg Bay', and St Margaret's Bay as 'Mahone Bay'.

It would seem a remarkable coincidence that Allen's legatee, Pickles, sought a pile of stones on the very island where Westhaver found the chart in a box within a cairn of stones. Who Allen was, and from where he obtained his chart, irrespective of its possible relevance to Oak Island, is an unfathomable mystery.

Whatever was the origin of the chart on which they were noted, Hedden had established that the direction printed by Wilkins fitted the markers on Oak Island 'Mr X's' most vital secret had been disclosed.

15 The Grand Design

Why did 'Mr X' require a marker system and directions, you may ask? The location of the treasure is obvious: it lies in the depths of the Money Pit, guarded by impregnable defences, the flooding that re-saturates the shaft at every high tide. I thought that – until I visited the island.

I stood by the shaft Hedden had dug in 1937 and looked into its murky depths. Thirty-three ft. down, the sea lapped the timbers of the old shoring. As the early searchers had dug down, the water surged up, flooding the shaft to tide-level and making its depths inaccessible, except, of course to Mr X who had provided himself with a convenient 'walk-in' tunnel! Its existence seems too improbable to warrant belief: anyone could stumble upon its entrance and, like the original shaft, the earth would have subsided. Mr X would not have thus jeopardized his concealment.

How, then, had he planned to recover his deposit? Not even Mr X himself could have beaten the flooding. He would not have put anything of value in the depths of a shaft which he *knew* would become flooded upon re-excavation.

He had been even more ingenious than we have realized. We know that Mr X harnessed the tides to protect his shaft. As the excavators dug down the sea surged up, reaching tide-level. Why had the water not seeped up previously?

As the early searchers dug downwards they encountered oaken platforms at each ten ft. level. Several of these platforms were sealed with layers of fibre, charcoal and putty. They were air-locks, preventing the water stored in the flood-tunnel from rising and flooding the Money Pit. The breaking of these locks allowed the air to escape, so the water rose within the Pit to within thirty-three ft. of the surface.

Johnson thinks Mr X dug deeper than he intended. He broke through the impervious clay into the porous strata below, through which, perhaps, flowed a subterranean stream. Thus he unwittingly increased the water-pressure and, consequently, the strength of his defences.

There are, however, objections to the 'air-lock' theory, as several correspondents have pointed out, following the serialization of my book in the London *Sunday Times*. Mr D. F. Gibbs of Bristol, England, doubts if the water in the flood tunnels could have been held down until 1804, when the air-seals were first broken. He says:

> If we assume that the water was in 1804 still below the lower spruce platform at 100 feet, the excess pressure would correspond to 65 feet of sea water, or about two atmospheres. It is difficult to believe that the cavity could be sufficiently well sealed with wood and putty to contain this pressure for 24 years. Compare, for example, the air in your car tyre, where the chance of making an airtight seal is comparatively good! It seems to me likely that even in the unlikely absence of gross leaks, the porosity of the wood and of the surrounding soil would be sufficient to release the air in weeks rather than years. Putty applied to the *top* of the platforms would not be a very effective seal with this sort of pressure, and it is difficult to see how it could have been applied to the under side. Perhaps some slow generation of gas could compensate the leakage, but I do not find it very credible.
>
> The other difficulty concerns the total upthrust on the platforms due to the rather large pressure. If the shaft were 13 feet in diameter all the way down, I estimate this as about 230 tons. I find it hard to believe that the wooden platforms would stand this at all, let alone for 24 years! I think there would be great difficulty in keying them into the walls of the pit sufficiently well, even if the wood itself were strong enough. I do not see any likely mechanism for distributing the upthrust more or less evenly between several platforms, for any length of time. However, if the diameter of the pit were reduced to a few feet near the bottom, the thrust might become manageable.
>
> A possible way round the air leakage problem, perhaps, is to assume that the air had been expelled sufficiently to let the water begin to penetrate at least one platform, when the rate of rise would be considerably reduced, by the greater density and viscosity of water compared to air, and perhaps because of the swelling of the wood and silting up of the cracks. However, a well made wooden boat, subject to much smaller pressure differences, usually requires baling out more frequently than once in 24 years!

I put Mr Gibbs's objection to another of my correspondents, Mr Patrick O'Connor, Lecturer in Soil Mechanics, Civil Engineering Department, Brighton Polytechnic, England. He has attempted to explain his opinion of the problem in very simplified form. From a technical point of view it would require considerable elaboration.

He believes that the 'plug' would have resisted the 'uplift' of water due to various factors – the sealed platforms in combination with the backfill between, formed of compacted clay which has a low permeability to water. 'The cohesion of the clay, together with the interaction of the platforms with the walls of the shaft, would have provided the net force necessary to stop the collapse into the void below of the clay backfill "plug".'

The balance of forces would have been sufficient to maintain the air pressure. Mr X's problem, O'Connor thinks, would have been to prevent the 'plug' from collapsing into the water-filled void below, rather than the other way about.

Mr John H. Haslett advances an even more ingenious explanation. He believes that the Money Pit was a magnificent piece of hydraulic engineering, unconnected with concealment. The fluctuating air pressure, increasing and decreasing as the tide rose and fell, constituted a 'pumping action':

The pressure of air trapped in the shaft holds back the waters of the ocean attempting to enter via the flood tunnels. It also holds back surface water draining through the soil which would otherwise seep through the walls of the shaft. The pressure will be communicated via the cellular structure of the clay soil, forcing back the water in the soil over a considerable area around the shaft. At high tide the water in the soil is forced further back by the increased air pressure. At low tide the water seeps down further through the soil, closer to the shaft. A vast area of soil around the shaft is being used as a sponge squeezed at high tide to give up some of its absorbed surface water, relaxed at low tide to draw in more water from the surface and surrounding areas.

When squeezed, water would rise in the soil, possibly oozing at the surface, certainly seeping through the walls of the upper part of the shaft, above the air-locks, to accumulate in the shaft to form a fresh-water well, replenished by natural drainage augmented by the pumping action of the compressed-air reservoir below. One would then expect to find a water-course leading from the well down to the beach at a point away from the Smith's Cove catchment, where fresh water could be collected in casks and loaded on boats for shipment to the mainland. Exactly such a water-course is described leading to the southern shore. The experiment with coloured dye, which appeared at the southern shore and not at Smith's Cove, suggests that the connection to the southern water-course is from the upper part of the pit.

In other words, Mr Haslett thinks that, as sinking a deep well in the rocky soil of Nova Scotia was impracticable, the off-shore island of clay, with its green foliage indicating an abundance of surface water was chosen to provide a permanent fresh-water supply. 'The unknown genius devised the scheme for hydraulic pumping, using the power of the ocean tides. That the air-locks held until broken open many years later bears witness to the skill of the designer and constructors of the shaft.'

Ingenious though Mr Haslett's explanation is, it seems unlikely that anyone would choose an island in a remote bay on which to provide a permanent well, especially as Nova Scotia is abundant in rivers, streams and lakes.

Whatever is the true explanation of the air-locks, it seems certain that there cannot be a sealed and water-tight chamber in the depths of the shaft. The Money Pit is not itself a treasure cache. But, it played a vital part in the Grand Design, Mr X's ingenious plan of concealment. This is what I think he did:

One gang dug the shaft by the old oak tree, its branch providing a useful hoist for the extraction of earth. As the workmen descended, they built platforms, connected by ladders, to facilitate lifting out the heavy soil.

It is possible, however, that Mr X found the shaft ready-made. Gwynne-Evans is a keen amateur geologist and he spent two months in the summer of 1965 touring around Mahone Bay. He thinks that Mr X may have found a sink-hole by the ancient oak tree.

Geologist E. Rudolph Faribault reached the same conclusion in 1911. In his *Summary Report of Geological Survey Branch of the Department of Mines*, he stated: 'There is strong evidence to prove that the supposed artificial openings (which originally led to the search) were really but natural sink holes and cavities formed by the gradual disillusion of gypsum deposits underlying layers of soft sandstone and shales which gave way under the pressure of the super-incumbent covering of glacial drift.'

109

Faribault, like Gwynne-Evans in 1965, found numerous deep sink-holes on the mainland adjacent to Oak Island.

Sink-holes or solution caverns, are cylindrical and funnel-shaped depressions. They often extend to great depths and lead to a labyrinth of cavities or caverns. The Carlsbad Caverns and the Kentucky Caves are famous examples.

Mahone Bay forms part of the Windsor Rock Formation and it suffers from its faulting and folding. Its stratigraphy is limestone, a formation which produces sink-holes and solution caverns. The Canadian Department of Mines Geological Survey (1929) shows that this limestone formation includes the eastern end but not the rest of Oak Island. Their Map 40 (1961) demonstrates that the island is affected by the Gold River Fault System.

It would not be surprising for a sink-hole to have formed on Oak Island. The fault which runs beneath the island could account for the underground stream which appears to run through the depths of the Money Pit. Talking to a reporter on 25 March 1966, geologist Robert Dunfield said, 'we have sufficient evidence of where the Windsor Formation is and this is the answer to the water problem'. The Money Pit site was, he thought, part of an underground natural rock structure of carbonate, as in minerals such as limestone.

Dunfield believed that the original depositors found a cavity at the bottom of the Pit which they made into a sealed and water-tight treasure chamber.

In 1942 Edwin Hamilton penetrated deeper into the Pit than any previous or subsequent searcher. He encountered an underground stream, but he did not remark any feature to support the solution cavern theory. He found no evidence to prove the existence of a treasure-chamber, whether man-made or of natural origin.

I neither accept nor reject Gwynne's theory. Whether or not Mr X found a ready-made shaft does not change my reconstruction of his Grand Design.

While one gang dug, or improved, the shaft, another excavated the beach at Smith's Cove, an undertaking which must have required the construction of a coffer-dam to hold back the tides. This gang made the fan-shaped drains and dug the sump-hole.

It remained to run the flood tunnel from the sump-hole

to the Pit, a distance of 500 ft. A succession of miners worked at its face as it progressed, each man throwing the spoil behind him for another to drag away. How did they keep the tunnel on line?

Mr X probably set his course by triangulation, using trigonometry. He had already set up his datum line by placing the two drilled rocks approximately twenty-five rods apart. They form a line seven degrees south of the True East-West line. The sump-hole lies on the same line as the drilled rocks, and about ten ft. inland from the beach. Its exact position can no longer be determined, due to the devastation in 1966 but I have located it according to the diagram, showing the fan drain, sump-hole and flood tunnel, drawn by Frederick Blair in 1895, and by my own measurements.

Reference to the Plan (page 98) shows that the line of the proposed tunnel lay fourteen degrees south of the True East-West line. That gave Mr X the bearing he needed. Standing at the sump-hole his compass needle pointed West. (He did not need to explain to his miners that he had allowed for magnetic variation.) He instructed them to 'steer' compass West, a cardinal point heavily marked. It is exactly the same as when navigating a ship, my son-in-law Hilary Watson explained. 'If you want to steer in a particular direction, you give the steersman a course which allows for magnetic variation.'

Mr X needed also to instruct his miners on the tunnel's gradient. The flood tunnel enters the Pit at 110 ft. The sump-hole is thought to have been seventy ft. deep. The operators, who in 1895 attempted to dynamite the flood tunnel, found it at eighty ft., approximately ten ft. inland from the sump-hole. The flood tunnel was 500 ft. in length. Thus the dip between the sump-hole and the Pit is forty ft., the gradient one ft. in twelve. How did the miners slope the tunnel downwards, or upwards if they started at the other end?

Mr J. P. F. O'Connor has suggested that it would have been extremely hazardous for the miners to have tunnelled from the Pit eastwards and upwards 'as their angle of dip would have been difficult to calculate accurately, and they might have emerged under the sea'.

Several methods were available in the eighteenth century. They are described by Professor Henry Briggs (*A Brief History of Mine Surveying*; Chapter xv, *Historical Review*

111

of Coal Mining, 1925). We cannot guess whether Mr X used any of these devices. He needed only a quadrant, 'a favourite levelling instrument for centuries', and a plumb line.

A quadrant is a quarter circle marked with ninety degrees with the plumb line hanging down from the vertical edge. The miner rotates the quadrant for the plumb line to indicate the predetermined number of degrees that gives the correct gradient. The number of degrees required would already have been calculated by trigonometry. Once he had started work, the miner would have needed to set up his quadrant, and look along its vertical edge, every few feet. As long as the plumb line indicated the correct number of degrees, he kept his gradient.

The flood tunnel must have taken a long time to dig. To make doubly sure, Mr X ran a second and deeper tunnel which entered the Pit at 150 ft.

The excavation of even one tunnel would have been a stupendous task. It is absurd to think that such an under-taking could have been achieved by amateurs, by pirates, or even by ordinary seamen or soldiers. It was an expert job which could have been accomplished only by experi-enced, disciplined miners.

The sump-hole and the Pit have been joined by two tunnels, each three and a half ft. high and two and a half ft. wide, and packed with beach stones. Mr X has dug his Pit, built his water catchment and run his flood tunnels. He does not yet connect the water supply to the shaft.

The final stage of Mr Xs Grand Design may have been planned to prevent his workmen from knowing the exact location of his cache or caches. This last operation could have been done by a selected few.

Mr X descends into the depths of the shaft. From its base his men tunnel upwards and outwards to create a cache, or caches, beneath the surface, above high-water mark, without disturbing the ground. He may have made several caches. He could return at his leisure, with even fewer men, and quickly recover one or more without re-vealing the whole plan of concealment.

Having made his caches, Mr X climbed from the shaft, his men refilled it with earth, sealing each platform down to ninety ft., and connecting the water supply. No one could ever go that way again; as they dug down, they would release the air-pressure and the sea would surge up and flood the shaft. The entrance to the treasure's hiding place was for ever sealed, Mr X's defences were impregnable, his treasure absolutely safe. The water would flow as long as the tides rolled up the beach.

Johnson, who reached the same conclusion independently – that Mr X dug upwards and outwards to establish his treasure cache some distance from the Pit – and I, derive some corroboration for our theory from the 'Spanish Sailor's' story which Frederick Blair heard in 1893. His correspondent had been told the story by an elderly relative who had met the sailor in his youth, possibly in the early years of the nineteenth century. The writer made no attempt to capitalize on his information, telling it merely as being possibly interesting. His relative recalled:

When a young man of about 20 years of age, and that is a long time ago, I was working in a shipyard when one day a sailor came into the yard. He was evidently from a foreign ship that had arrived to load deal, as the place was a great resort then for ships in the lumber trade. He was a man of about 50 years of age, large, heavy, dark and swarthy. I entered into conversation with him. He said he was anxious to raise some money to enable him to get back to Boston, that if I would advance say $20.00 he in return would give me a valuable secret of where there was an immense amount of money buried. He then told me something of his history. That he had been a pirate, and in later years a privateer, and that now as the latter occupation was about played out, he was getting weary and wanted to get home to his native country, Spain. That if he could get to Boston he would stand a better chance of finding a ship going there. He showed me a plan which he said had come into his possession, and the meaning of which he could clearly explain. It was of an island of a certain form, situated on the south-western coast of Nova Scotia and was once a rendezvous of pirates, and that a large amount of treasure was buried there.

On this island was a certain oak tree, from a branch of which hung a large ship's block which was used in sinking a deep shaft, the bottom of which communicated with the sea level by a tunnel. The shaft had been filled up as being of no use, as the exit for the removal of the treasure would be through the tunnel. But for reasons unknown to him the treasure was never put there, but buried only 20 feet from the surface, at a certain distance from the tree, naming the distance, where it would be safer from the inquisitive intruder than if it were at the bottom of the shaft, the most likely place to look for it, and then it may have been the original intention of the depositor that the shaft was intended for a blind, for who would not be deceived under such conditions.

When the sailor had finished his story, I, as you can imagine, was worked up to a high pitch of curiosity to find out where this wonderful island was, but on this point hinged our bargain. When I paid him the money he was to give me the name and directions how to find the island, also to mark on the plan the exact course by compass from the tree that the treasure lay buried, so that having found the island, then the tree with the course and directions given, it would be an easy matter to find the spot, when a few days digging would reveal the wonderful collection of untold wealth. Yes, of course, I would agree to his offer and the money would be forthcoming next day.

Sleep that night to me was long delayed, it was to dream of finding the precious coins and feasting my eyes on the glittering gold. The next day, however, when I came to look at the matter from various points of reason, my ardour cooled somewhat. The story seemed too good to be true. It savoured too much of the improbable. Besides it was a good deal of money for me to raise at that time. So I wavered all day undecided what to do, until the following day. When that day came the sailor disappeared as suddenly as he had come. I learned that he left in a vessel for Eastport and from there to Boston.

The story-teller regretted his want of decision, stated Blair's correspondent, when, in after years, he heard about the parties digging on Oak Island which 'corresponded in so many points with that described by the pirate sailor'. He believed that his story referred to that place.

The letter writer went on to say, 'This is the end of my relative's story. I may say that in answer to questions put by myself, he said that the pirate did not associate Captain Kidd's name in any way whatever with the business, and furthermore that he placed the date of the deposit at about the close of the last century. My relative also attributes considerable importance to a large rock as being an important landmark.'

Blair, who was living in Boston at the time, failed to locate his correspondent.

The sailor could not have learned, before 1850, that a tunnel connected the Money Pit to the sea and the possibility that a 'large rock' formed an important landmark was not disclosed until 1937 when Hedden found the drilled rocks and the stone triangle. The remarkable feature of the story is the statement that the deposit was made some distance from the tree, and not in the shaft which was intended as a blind. That theory was first advanced, and then privately, in 1960.

The Spanish sailor had shown what lawyers call 'guilty knowledge'. He appears to have known something which he could not have even suspected unless he had been personally concerned in the operation, or had heard it, in garbled form, perhaps, from someone who had been there.

The sailor admitted to having been a pirate and a privateer. He may have served in the latter capacity during the War of American Independence (1775-82), the latest period in that century when a man of his likely age could have served on a privateer in American waters. He may have been a sailor on one of the vessels which brought the workmen to Oak Island, or he may have gleaned his information from one of them; he spoke of a plan which had '*come*' into his possession. His story sounds as if he had heard talk which he did not fully understand and it gains authenticity from its lack of precise detail.

Neither Johnson nor I present the Spanish sailor as a 'witness of truth': his story may reflect an early oral tradition; it would have been surprising if none of the workmen had talked.

Mr X's plan was perfect. It remained only to mark on the ground the spots below which his men had tunnelled. That is why he required a marker system. He devised a code to fit the markers for easy memorization, to record the 'way back', should he need to send an heir or deputy to recover the treasure. I need to delay their discussion in order to explain Roy Reynish's ingenious theory.

At one of our many talks Reynish remarked, 'You know, "Mr X" did not need to go as far as the Money Pit. He could have made a safe concealment nearer the shore, requiring only a short flood tunnel. He could have dug sideways and upwards from it and placed his cache close to the surface. Once the water had been connected, the entrance was for ever sealed.'

Reynish was not presenting a theoretical hypothesis. He was attempting to explain the existence of what is known as the 'Cave-In' shaft. It was found accidentally in 1878.

Mrs Henry Sellers, it will be recalled, helped her father, Anthony Graves, with his farming on the island. While ploughing about 350 ft. east of the Money Pit and about 150 ft. from the shore at Smith's Cove, her two oxen fell into a 'well-like' hole. The beasts were rescued with difficulty. This 'cave-in' occurred above the supposed line of the flood-tunnel. Her husband, Sellers, filled the hole with boulders. (Frederick Blair and his partner Robert Creelman, explored this in 1895.)

Removal of the boulders revealed a well-defined shaft six to eight ft. in diameter and fifteen to eighteen ft. deep. It was considered to be part of the original work, constructed at the same time as the Money Pit. The discovery that the shaft's walls were so hard that it was difficult to drive a pick into them seemed to prove this. The workmen excavated to the depth of fifty-two ft. from where a boring was made to the depth of sixteen ft. without result. Next morning, water broke into the shaft, reaching mean-tide level. This water was assumed to come from another searcher's shaft more than 200 ft. away. It had been sunk in 1850 at a distance of 140 ft. eastwards of the Money Pit, to the depth of seventy-five ft., when *no* water had been encountered in it.

Blair is infuriatingly vague about this Cave-In shaft; 'As the cribbing was located partly in new ground and partly in old ground, the pressure became unequal and the shaft was declared unsafe for the workmen and was abandoned'. When the Cave-In shaft was reopened to fifty-two ft. in 1896, salt water broke in at that depth. Blair explained, 'Eventually they [the workmen] got into a tunnel which measured four feet by six feet and was well timbered, but it turned out to be a tunnel driven by the operators in 1866-67, and not the pirate [i.e. flood] tunnel. Their calculations indicated that the pirate tunnel was probably not more than five feet below this tunnel, which struck one side of the Cave-In shaft.'

The records of the operations at Cave-In shaft are ambiguous. We only learn that a tunnel, whoever had driven it, struck one side of the shaft above the fifty-two ft. level. The Cave-In shaft became filled with water, although the flood tunnel was assumed to run, at that place, five ft. deeper. That assumption was clearly incorrect.

At that place, 150 ft. from the beach, the flood tunnel must lie at the depth of eighty-two ft. Thus, the bottom of the Cave-In shaft, at fifty-two ft., must be thirty-two ft. above it. Yet, sea-water broke into it from somewhere, and its base could be reached by a tunnel leading from the beach.

Blair appears to have dismissed the possibility that this shaft may have been dug by the operators in 1867 in an abortive attempt to reach and intercept the flood tunnel. There is no record that they excavated at that unlikely spot. It would have been far easier to trace the tunnel close to the beach at a point where it reached nearer the surface.

On very slight evidence, the Cave-In shaft was explained as an air-vent, constructed by the original depositors to facilitate the digging of the flood tunnel. Although Blair thought it 'might be the key to the problem', no further work was undertaken at the site until 1940 when Edwin Hamilton explored beneath and around its base. Descending through a shaft near Smith's Cove, Hamilton crawled along a tunnel which curved gradually, and divided, 'going both sides' of the Cave-In shaft. Below this tunnel, he found another, and deeper still, yet another tunnel. This deeper tunnel lay in perfect line above the flood tunnel.

In the floor of this third tunnel, Hamilton sank a shaft eleven ft. deep, encountering sand, beach gravel, small stones and blue clay but no water. About six ft. down he unearthed a large flat stone, not native to that level, and alongside it, several pieces of chewing leaf tobacco in good state of preservation, left apparently by the old diggers. At the ten ft. level he came across bits of wood and twigs which gave 'the appearance of an old trench dug from the top down to flood the Money Pit', which lay more than 300 ft. to the west. One of these tunnels 'extended under the beach'.

Hamilton explored several other tunnels beneath the small hill which rises between the beach and the Money Pit, and others close to Smith's Cove. He concluded that they had been driven by the Halifax Company in 1867, despite the silence of that Company's foreman, Fraser, on that subject. It is inconceivable that the Halifax men could have dug the shafts and driven the tunnels that have been attributed to them.

Hamilton told me that, though the Cave-In shaft was full of surface water, no water percolated down into the double tunnel beneath it. That tunnel lay 'considerably above' the flood-tunnel. Yet the flood-tunnel was not all that much deeper for, when the pumps at the Money Pit stopped working, water bubbled up through the floor of the tunnel he was in.

Hamilton's exploration seems to establish that the Cave-In shaft ended well above the flood-tunnel. How then could it have served as an air-vent?

The question whether an air-vent would have been required or not has been argued with some asperity, chiefly by people inexperienced in subterranean tunnelling. Alarik Walton, for example, contends that at least two air-vents would have been necessary to ventilate a 500 ft. long tunnel. The Cave-In shaft, 150 ft. from the beach, was one, and another may lie still undiscovered at 300 ft. He places reliance on the fact that the Cave-In shaft lies at approximately one third of the distance from the beach to the Pit. I advance two reasons why an air-vent was not made: by excavating above the flood-tunnel, Mr X would have jeopardized his defences; trespassers might have found it and used it to block off the water at that point; and why was an air-vent not required to carry fresh air into the far deeper, lower flood-tunnel?

My researches show that old-time miners had devised another method to ventilate their tunnels. It was employed by James Brindley in 1765, in digging a mile-long tunnel at Worsley, near Manchester, England. He erected at its mouth a water-bellows for 'the purpose of forcing fresh air into the interior and thus ventilating the works'. He described the apparatus; (*St James Chronicle*, 30 September 1763) thus:

> At the mouth of the cavern is erected a water-bellows being the body of a tree, forming a hollow-cylinder, standing upright. Upon this a wooden bason is fixed, in the form of a funnel, which receives a current of water from the higher ground. The water falls into the cylinder, and issues out at the bottom of it, but at the same time carries a quantity of air with it, which is received into the pipes and forced into the innermost recess in the coal pits, where it issues out as if from a pair of bellows, and rarifies the body of thick air which would otherwise prevent the workmen from subsisting on the spot where the coals are dug.

Reynish's theory may supply a more convincing answer to

the question of the purpose of the Cave-In shaft. Having run his flood-tunnel for 150 ft., Mr X dug sideways and upwards, in order to create a cache close to and beneath the surface. Once he had 'turned on the tap', the entrance was blocked. If he did that, it remained to mark the spot on the surface. Here I take over from Reynish.

It is possible that Mr X did mark that spot although it is uncertain because the exact site of the Cave-In shaft can no longer be determined, having disappeared during Dunfield's excavations. Hedden told me that 'Roper slightly misplaced it' on his Survey, correcting it in subsequent prints. about the shaft's exact position. He thinks it is slightly south of the point, seven rods from the Easterly Drilled Rock, and does not lie directly above the supposed line of the flood tunnel. Roper was asked only to plot the Directions. Another contemporary source states that 'on this line (of the Drilled Rocks) at a point seven rods from one rock and eighteen from the other, they (Roper and Hedden) found the Cave-In shaft'. This conflicts with the Survey on which Roper placed the Cave-In shaft about ten to fifteen ft. to the south-east of that point.

The so-called 'point', seven rods from the Easterly Drilled Rock, and eighteen from the Westerly Drilled Rock is in fact a space nine ft. in width.

Roper, we recall, found the two rocks to lie, not 412 ft. apart, the exact equivalent of twenty-five rods, but $421\frac{1}{2}$ ft. – nine ft. in excess. This discrepancy puzzled me. It seemed strange that the precise Mr X had left nine ft. 'in the air' so to speak. He could easily have placed the two rocks exactly 412 ft. apart and he took great care to get them exactly in line. (The drilled holes may have supported sticks to enable a person, standing on the hill between, to check their position.)

Did Mr X intend to leave that nine ft. gap? It would have been a convenient method for marking a spot, eighteen rods from one rock and seven from the other.

The possibility that Mr X may have left the 'gap' to mark a spot underground enhances, but does not prove, Reynish's theory that he could have tunnelled upwards at that point to establish his treasure cache, or one of them at least.

Reynish's theory appears to be supported by the silence of the directions to the Westerly Drilled Rock. Thus, they could equally apply to the line between the Money Pit and the Easterly Drilled Rock, the distance between the two points being the same. That is also approximately the line of the flood-tunnel. If that is the true explanation, gap and flood-tunnel would coincide.

Thus if Reynish is right, it means that Mr X.:

1 Either continued his flood-tunnel for a further 350 ft., to the Money Pit, to provide an entrance for further caches, or the Money Pit was a blind.
2 He added to the Directions, recording instructions to go '30. S.W.' etc., to distract attention from the nine ft. gap between the two Drilled Rocks.
3 He returned to recover his deposit from the 'Cave-In' shaft.

Having dug downwards at the site of the 'gap', he refilled the hole. The earth subsided leaving a hard crust or arch of earth on the surface which collapsed under the weight of the two oxen. (Old Roman wells have been found in England by the collapse of such a crust. I heard of an example at Findon, Sussex, in 1965.) There is no evidence that Mr X dug up further deposits. No early searcher or resident remarked disturbed or recessed ground other than that beneath the ancient oak tree.

I find it hard to believe that Mr X would have run his flood-tunnel for a further 350 ft., and have excavated his deep shaft by the tree for no other purpose than to serve as a decoy. I prefer to think it was his 'main entrance' for other caches.

Johnson and I differ where these caches may lie. He relies solely on the marker system which he considers to be clear and precise; 'Mr X did not need a code.' I think that Mr X devised the code, the Directions printed by Wilkins, to enable his deputy or heir to interpret the markers. It would have served as a memory aid to the man to whom he had explained his Grand Design, and its starting point.

Johnson has explained why he believes Mr X tunnelled upwards to a certain point and how he laid his course. I cannot disclose his ingenious theory. I disagree only when he claims it is the only possible explanation of the markers. In 1962, he drilled five holes on the line of the supposed upward tunnel. He encountered what he called a 'bewildering thing'. His heavy pneumatic drills, which are designed to blow the drilled material back up a hole, encountered so much mud 'that the air could not blow the thick stuff back up out of the hole'. With the drill shut off, Johnson could still hear the air being pumped down through the drill pipe. 'The ground was so dreadfully hard that it is difficult to imagine anything passing through it'. When the compressor was shut off, the air continued to boil up violently for some time. He says:

> It appeared to us that we must have pumped a large quantity of air into a cavity or void, probably displacing the water which previously filled the void, and that on shutting off the compressor it took 45 minutes for the displaced water to force its way back in and displace the air. During further drilling along the general line where I believe the treasure tunnel lies, we had air passing from hole to hole and even to our 1962 shaft, and this over a distance of nearly 100 feet.

Johnson believed that this experience confirmed his choice of the particular site.

Reynish and I were puzzled by the Triangle. The Directions did not mention it. Roper's course from the two Drilled Rocks fell below its base, whereas it might have been expected to strike either its base or its Apex Stone. Fortunately, Hedden or Blair had drawn the Triangle; Johnson had inspected it, finding the Apex Stone marked with a cross, and Summers had photographed it before its removal or obscuration by Dunfield.

It was very rough. It was built of beach stones spaced apart. Each side and the base was ten ft. long. Its base angles were connected by a curved line made of six stones. From this curved line ran an arrow of stones; it intersected the base of the triangle, four ft. from one side and six ft. from the other, and continued on through the Apex Stone.

It is important to explain that this arrow is not a median line – a perpendicular line drawn from the centre of the base through the apex. It runs left of centre. It points True North, whereas the Triangle is cocked 6° 35′ West of North.

The Triangle seems to have served a very significant, if not obvious, purpose, which requires discussion later.

From the point reached by following the course '30 S.W.' below the Triangle's base, the Directions continue '14 N.

Tree'. Roper, we recall, when he set up his sights, noticed that the stone arrow pointed directly at the Money Pit, by which, once stood the ancient and conspicuous oak tree. But '14 rods' or 231 ft. is not the true distance to the Pit. From the Triangle's base it is 295 ft.

The final figures in the Directions are mystifying. They read '7 By 8 By 4'.

I thought I had found it when I noticed that the stones which form the 'westerly' side of the Triangle numbered seven, counting downwards from the Apex Stone. Eight stones formed the base and four stones lay between one point of the base and the arrow. On that basis the cryptic numbers seemed to indicate the 'triangle within the triangle' formed by the arrow of stones. This somewhat dubious conclusion led nowhere in particular, other than, perhaps, to confirm that the Directions pointed north on the line of the arrow. I tried another explanation. When the boys discovered the Pit in 1795, they found a layer of flag stones four ft. down. Could these figures have indicated the dimensions of the shaft? Seven ft. one way, eight ft. another, and four ft. down? I place no great reliance on this interpretation either.

Reynish and I experimented with these figures on the basis that they constituted a triangle, its three sides being respectively 7, 8 and 4 rods. Clearly, the unit of measurement could not have been changed without identification. Reaching the point indicated by '14 (Rods) N. Tree', we built the triangle as 4 rods (the remaining distance to the Money Pit, on the line of the tunnel, and 8 rods from the starting point. The triangle's apex appeared thus to indicate a position above the flood tunnel. The likelihood that it marked a cache seemed improbable for the record of the early searchers' excavations shows that several shafts had been dug in that area in attempts to intercept the flood tunnel. Alternatively, the triangle could be projected westward of the Money Pit, with the same disappointing result. One of my correspondents believes he has found a connection of sorts between these figures and the head of the Death Valley on Wilkins's map. He takes encouragement from the Biblical admonition, 'Yea, though I walk through the Valley of Death, Thy rod and staff shall comfort me', and 'Goodness and mercy shall follow'.

Another correspondent, an ex-Sapper, thinks that the '7

By 8 By 4' represents in feet or yards the size of the treasure chamber, and another believes that the cryptogram is a sort of geometrical conjuring trick, a delusion to conceal the true answer, consistent with the general camouflage and deception shown by the Pit's designer.

I doubt the validity of any of these explanations. Had Wilkins, I wondered, added these cryptic figures to the directions he had received from Westhaver?

I have interpreted the markers and code to indicate a certain spot. The prolonged activities of the Triton Alliance have delayed my search. If I find nothing I shall not be disappointed. I am more concerned to identify 'Mr X', and learn why he laboured so diligently.

16 The Year of Genius

Who was he? His Grand Design proves Mr X to have been a genius of engineering and of guile. He had a strange and subtle imagination and a bizarre sense of humour. He seems to have enjoyed the thought that his shaft might be found, his defences put to test. He went to considerable lengths to mask his identity. But he could not help leaving certain clues.

He used the ancient English unit of measure, the rod, in his code, which suggests English or English-Colonial origin. His use of that unit, however, to define the course to be followed does not necessarily imply that he laid out his works in rods.

There were two methods available. Mr X could have used Gunter's Chain of a hundred links and sixty-six ft. in length, invented in 1632. Having measured his distances he might have converted them into rods to eliminate fractions. For example, the distance of eighteen rods from the Westerly Drilled Rock is the equivalent of 4.50 chains. Seven rods from the Easterly Drilled Rock equals 1.75 chains. It may have been simpler to record the directions in whole numbers.

Or he may have laid out his works by true bearings, by triangulation. His choice of method could well have been conditioned by the ground. It rises between the two Drilled Rocks, obscuring one from the other. Other than around the ancient oak tree, by the shaft, his view would have been further obscured by the dense growth, of oak trees. This may have prevented measurement by triangulation. It would have been easier to lay a chain on the ground, through the trees and over the small hill.

Whether or not the method of measurement provides a clue to the nationality of the man who designed the works, the word 'Rock' used in the directions may point to his origin. Surely an Englishman would have employed the word 'stone'?

I consulted several dictionaries. A modern American uses

the word 'rock' when he means a stone small enough to throw. (H. Wentworth, *American Dialect Dictionary*, 1944.) But that was not always so. H. L. Mencken (*The American Language*, 1947) shows that the Puritans built *rocks* into the foundations of their meeting houses as early as 1712. They rejected the word 'stone' as having a sexual implication. The use of the word 'rock' may not however be as useful as it sounds. 'Rock', I am told, is a common and correct terminology in civil engineering, and 'stone' is employed in a particular sense, such as in 'Portland' stone.

Mr X could not help disclosing a more significant clue. Probably it never occurred to him that anyone would spot it. Can the works be dated by the magnetic variation of the compass that operated at the time?

The declination of the compass varies slowly with time and is different in different places. At any time, anywhere, the magnetic variation will be at variance with True, or Geographical North.

Suspecting that magnetic variation might be the key to the puzzle, I wrote to the Division of Geomagnetism, Department of Mines, Ottawa. They sent me *The March of the Compass in Canada* (*The Canadian Surveyor*, Vol. XXI, No. 5, December 1967). Its authors, Edward Dawson and L. C. Dalgethy, stated: 'The direct approach is by far the best when using old magnetic bearings to determine the present bearings of old property lines. In this method, it is necessary to identify one of the lines and observe its compass bearings; the differences between the present bearing and the one recorded in the deed can then be applied to other old bearings.'

Reynish and I drew our own plan, based on the Roper survey, and incorporating other information and measurements, such as the true position of the Money Pit, about which Roper had been misinformed. Colin Summers and W. L. Johnson had independently measured the 'cant' of the Stone Triangle, finding it to be 6° 35' west of north. Johnson believed it had been canted originally seven degrees. Its stones had become warped from weathering and time.

Various facts emerged from our Plan. The line of the Drilled Rocks lies seven degrees south of the True East-West line. The line joining the Easterly Drilled Rock and the Money Pit (indicated by the Hedden shaft) forms an-

125

other seven-degree angle. Together they make a fourteen-degree angle.

These lines and angles suggested that the works had been laid out in a year when the compass variation was 14° west of north. They are shown on the Plan drawn by Roy Reynish and executed for this book by Hilary Watson. He is a yacht designer, a draftsman and sailor. When I put our reasoning to him Watson said he thought it would be impossible to prove conclusively that any ancient works, or land boundaries, had been laid out according to any particular magnetic variation by the occurrence of certain angles which might show half the declination. To prove that the Oak Island works had been laid out in a year when the variation was fourteen degrees, it would be necessary to recognize one contemporary compass bearing. Several days later we were discussing how Mr X ran his flood tunnel from the sump-hole to the Money Pit. Its course disclosed that Mr X knew that the current variation was fourteen. He directed his miners to 'steer' compass west.

Later Watson came up with a convincing explanation for the Stone Triangle. His reasoning was as follows:

The direction of the flood tunnel, connecting sump-hole and Money Pit, was Mr X's greatest problem. His miners would be working in a cramped, dimly lit space, burrowing for 500 ft. He needed to make it easy for them to follow the correct course, to strike the Money Pit exactly. They could do that by following their compass needle, provided that he gave them the right directions.

First, he needed to establish the prevailing magnetic variation. Due to proximity to the Pole, and consequent erratic swings, it was necessary to establish the current mean value by permanent record.

Mr X established his base line by placing, or finding in position, two rocks which lay roughly on an east-west line. To establish the true bearing of that line, he set up a 'sun-compass', a specialized type of sun-dial.

The sun-compass was a recognized sixteenth-century navigational device, incorporated in a box, in which an upright style cast a shadow on a dial at forenoon and afternoon altitudes of the sun. It enabled the navigator to determine true north by daylight, and the current magnetic variation. The variation so established could be applied to any subsequent magnetic compass bearing in order to convert it to true or geographical direction.

By constructing the Stone Triangle, Mr X provided himself with a permanent sun-compass. He may have drawn his design on paper before transferring it to the ground where his sight may have been obscured by trees and contour.

He selected a position directly south of the Westerly Rock, at a spot as near as possible to the southern shore in order to benefit from uninterrupted sunlight. There he laid down a line of stones which (when the Triangle was later constructed) became the arrow of stones intersecting base line and apex, pointing true north, and at the Westerly Rock and Money Pit.

He stands on the arrow of stones, facing the Westerly Rock. He sends a man walking westward from that rock, keeping the two rocks in line by means of sticks inserted into the drilled holes. The man halts and signals when the line between him and Mr X makes a right-angle with the projected base line between the two rocks. He fixes a stake in the ground.

Mr X measures the angle between the arrow of stones, which points true north, and the stake. It is seven degrees. The base line must therefore bear exactly the same angle, seven degrees south of the true east-west line. To permanently record this information, Mr X constructs the Stone Triangle, so that its 'cock' points directly at the stake at the projections of the base line. He can now plot the line of the flood tunnel from the sump-hole to the Money Pit, the position of which is fixed by the prominent oak tree.

He sends another man walking eastwards from the Easterly Rock near the beach at Smith's Cove, to establish the position of the sump-hole. He stops when the angle between the base line and the line to the Money Pit reaches seven degrees. The line from the sump-hole to the Money Pit must be fourteen degrees south of the true east-west line. That knowledge, so carefully worked out and recorded, enables Mr X to give his miners the correct and easy course to follow, i.e. compass west, a cardinal point heavily marked.

Mr X has shown professional skill and care in double referencing should the position of the two rocks become disturbed. Had he relied on his memory, the date when he did the job might never have been detected. But he has

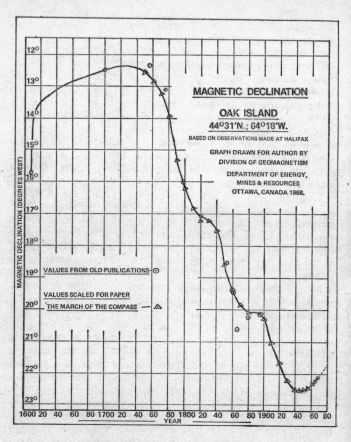

MAGNETIC DECLINATION

OAK ISLAND
44°31'N.; 64°18'W.

BASED ON OBSERVATIONS MADE AT HALIFAX

GRAPH DRAWN FOR AUTHOR BY
DIVISION OF GEOMAGNETISM

DEPARTMENT OF ENERGY,
MINES & RESOURCES
OTTAWA, CANADA 1968.

MAGNETIC DECLINATION (DEGREES WEST)

VALUES FROM OLD PUBLICATIONS⊙

VALUES SCALED FOR PAPER
THE MARCH OF THE COMPASS △

YEAR

now disclosed that he laid out his works in a year when the
magnetic variation of the compass was fourteen degrees west
of north.

Thus, we need to find a year or years when that variation
occurred.

The Division of Geomagnetism informed me that the
magnetic values for Nova Scotia went back to the year 1750.
Earlier values are extrapolated, and their reliability is uncertain. They sent me a graph giving the estimated values for
Oak Island. The value of fourteen degrees operated at two

dates, in 1780 and at a guess, about 1611. The year 1780 is confirmed by the chart of Mahone Bay drawn in 1773 by Des Barres (*Atlantic Neptune*). He noted the variation 13° 30′. The variation had risen to twenty-three degrees in 1937, the date of Roper's survey.

My curiosity about the Kidd charts, which are dated 1669, also led me to write to the Royal Observatory at Herstmonceux Castle, Sussex. They referred me to the work of W. van Bemmelen (*Magnetic and Meteorological Observations at Batavia*, Vol. XXI, 1898) and stated: 'An observation of 14° W. in 1669 would not be inconsistent with van Bemmelen's charts, but it would not be possible to decide the likely date of the observation within about 100 years, even if the observation itself were not likely to be in error by $+/- 2°$.'

Edmund Halley's Chart, the Astronomer Royal remarked, gave a more reliable value of 12° W for Nova Scotia in 1700. Halley crossed the Atlantic for his study of magnetism.

The value of 14° west for Oak Island in 1780 is reliable. The choice of that date for the origin of the works is supported by other, independent pieces of evidence.

The boys who found the shaft in 1795 remarked that, in the area surrounding the ancient oak tree, 'the first growth of wood had been cut down and another was springing up to supply its place. And some old stumps of oak trees that had been chopped down were visible.'

Unreliable as such a vague description must be, it suggests nonetheless that the fresh growth had not reached any great height. The expression 'springing up' suggests a height less than that of the observers. Oaks, I am told by the Chief Forester on the estate where I live in England, grow slowly at first, reaching three ft. after five to seven years, and six ft. after fifteen years. From twenty ft. the rate of growth is about one ft. per year. In the climate of Nova Scotia the rate could vary.

The clearing was still obvious; that is the important conclusion. The old oaks had been chopped down, and the new growth had started, not all that number of years before 1795. The boys' observation seems to rule out the possibility that the ground had been cleared much before 1780.

I wondered whether the condition of the branch which

had been cut short could also provide a clue. The Royal Forestry Society of England and Wales replied to my query, 'Oak is more durable against fungus than any other species and it is quite possible that a stump branch may still be found dead but not necessarily decayed after a hundred years.' Chief Forester John Rowe, however, thought that a lopped branch would tend to wither, and finally drop off after twenty to thirty years.

Attempts have been made to assess the age of this ancient oak which disappeared early in the search. It is assumed to have been about 200 years old in 1795. The life span of red oaks is about 250 years, by which time a tree might have attained a diameter of sixteen to eighteen ins. It would have been strong enough for a branch to have been used as a hoist after about one hundred years of growth. These conclusions serve only to limit the period in which the work could have been done. It carries us back to about the year 1695 as the earliest possible date.

There is another possible date indicator. The airlock, which prevented the upthrust of the sea-water in the shaft, is unlikely to have held indefinitely. Whatever is the true answer to this complicated matter, it is reasonable to conclude that the 'plug' was formed not all that long before it was broken by the early excavators.

These clues combine to indicate that the work was done about 1780 – the middle of the War of American Independence.

The British Army in North America numbered, at times, 35,000 men. They included a corps of military engineers, officers, artificers and a company of Cornish miners.

Much about Oak Island is uncertain, but one thing is sure – the work of digging and tunnelling could have been done only by a skilled and disciplined force, directed by an experienced engineer and surveyor.

Several correspondents have remarked on the professional nature of the job. Major R. A. Linton, RE (retired), considers that, 'Ingenious tunnel systems like this are typical of the sapper mentality.' He believes that, though designed as a concealment, the Money Pit was never used. The longitudinal section and plan of the works, thinks Mr O'Connor, is indicative only of trained engineering '*modus operandi*', and the 'field book plotting' of lengths and bearings from fixed observation points (e.g. 18 W and by 7 E on Rock) is consistent with good engineering thinking. No decent engineer, he believes, would put down any bore-hole, shaft or indeed any form of construction, without recording some fixed points from which a triangulation (or trilateration) could be made, at a later date, to the point, or points, under consideration. It would be in accordance with engineering psychology to construct a safe in the ground which could only be opened by following a set pattern.

Mr O'Connor agrees that the final stage of the operations would have been to connect the sump-hole to the catchment area. 'Thus the lock would have been effectively applied.' It was imperative to unlock the safe in the correct sequence of events. The first stage of the recovery operation would have been to dam the catchment, thus cutting off the water supply. Any civil engineering construction carried out under such a large hydraulic lead would be tricky, and would require an operational sequence to be followed implicitly.

The design of the Money Pit 'hideaway' was the work of a skilful engineer's shrewd brain, thinks Mr J. Follows Smith, a surveyor. Ex-Royal Engineer Linton, with whom I discussed Mr X's character, believes that he was the 'odd man out', the quiet, efficient craftsman who, when asked to do a job, did it thoroughly, to the astonishment, and sometimes the chagrin, of his more haphazard superiors. His familiarity with hydraulic engineering has suggested to several of my correspondents that he may have been a Cornishman who learned his techniques in tin-mining. Whatever his background, Mr X knew his job, as events have proved. No one has succeeded in unlocking the safe he so painstakingly constructed about the year 1780.

Some investigators, Johnson for example, object to so late a date, on the grounds that the town of Chester, four miles across the bay, had been founded in 1759. Surely the occupation of Oak Island by a large force, and the possible presence across the bay of several ships, could not have gone unnoticed? After the Pit's discovery in 1795, surely someone would have recalled unusual activity on the uninhabited island only fifteen years before?

It seems that someone did. The boys who discovered the shaft in 1795 were told that the island was haunted: fires had been seen at night and a party of men had rowed over and had not returned. This incident could not have occurred before 1759 when Chester was founded.

The presence in the bay of a British Military and Naval force in war-time may not have seemed strange. Like the 'dog that did not bark' in the Sherlock Holmes' story, *Silver Blaize*, the people of Chester may have failed to remark it. Fearful as they were of rebel raiders, they would not have failed to notice the presence of foreigners in the bay. Many of the men had been 'called-up' to help build and garrison the Citadel at Halifax (Harry Piers, *The Evolution of the Halifax Fortress, 1749-1928*, Publication, No. 7. The Public Archives of Nova Scotia, 1947).

The policy of mutual defence also operated in reverse. Beamish Murdock (*History of Nova Scotia*, 3 vols. 1865) states that on 4 June 1779, a sergeant and twelve soldiers were sent from Halifax to Chester to provide a garrison, as several vessels had been seized by rebel privateers. On 15 March, 1782, the Boston privateer, *Captain Potter*, captured the schooner *Two Sisters* in Mahone Bay. On 20 June and 1 July, enemy privateers landed ninety men and seized the town of Lunenburg, which was harassed again in August.

One personal record of American depredations at Chester survives (Historical Manuscripts Commission. *Report on American Manuscripts in the Royal Institution of Great Britain*, Vol. III):

JOHN NEWTON, CASPER WOLLENHAUPT, and OTTO WM. SCHWART to SIR A. S. HAMMOND, Lieutenant Governor of Nova Scotia. N. D. (1782) – Memorial Narrating that on the 1st of July last (no year stated, but this happened in 1782) a party of 90 men under the command of Lieutenant Batterman landed from five privateers at a place called Red Head, two miles distant, and entered the town by surprise at 1 o'clock in the morning, the privateers sailed up in front of the town. The principal part of the inhabitants were then at Halifax, those remaining were taken prisoners, Colonel Creighton having only time to get 6 men with himself into the Block House, which he defended between two and three hours until the privateers came abreast and fired, when he was obliged to surrender. The Captain of one of the privateers, whose name was Babcock and who had command of the party on shore, sent Wollenhaupt with a flag to the militia, who were then assembling, to say that if no opposition was made they would only take the merchandize in the town and would not injure buildings in town, which was acquiesced to. Having plundered everything to the amount of about 10,000l., they got on board their vessels and then demanded a ransom of 7,000l. for the town, but agreed to take 1,000l., for which memorialists were obliged to give a promissory note payable to Noah Stoddard captain of the largest privateer. The block house and Colonel Creighton's dwelling house were burnt, the guns spiked and the small arms carried away. Pray for a captain, two sub-alterns, and fifty British troops to be stationed with a hundred stand of small arms and ammunition for use of the militia.

Casper Wollenhaupt, a merchant of Chester, was an early grantee of land on Oak Island.

Mahone Bay was well known in 1780. It had been surveyed three times: first, by Charles Morris in 1762; followed in 1768 by the British military engineer, John Montrésor whose chart of Mahone Bay identified, but does not name, Oak Island. Des Barres, another military engineer, surveyed the bay in 1773.

I have taken great interest in Montrésor and Des Barres, because both men were capable of designing and constructing the island's works. I do not think that either did; Des Barres went to England in 1774 and Montrésor in 1778, their active careers being spent in North America.

Montrésor was born on 6 April 1736 and died on 26 June 1799. Part of his Journals have been published (New York Historical Society, *Collections for 1881*, N.Y. 1882), and he has been the subject of a short biography (J. C. Webster, *The Life of John Montrésor*. Transactions of the Royal Society of Canada, Series III, vol. XXII). I learned additional details from Colonel John Montrésor, his direct descendant, and from Lieutenant Colonel F. T. Stear, Secretary of the Royal Engineer Historical Society. The bulk, and the vital part as far as we are concerned, of Montrésor's Journals have not survived. (He lost his baggage six times, and his possessions were twice destroyed by fire.) As a result we know nothing about his survey of Mahone Bay.

John Montrésor became one of the Chief Engineers in America in 1775, commanding a battalion of six officers and artificers. He was present at the battle of Lexington in 1775 and lived in Boston during the siege that winter. Following the British evacuation of the city in May 1776, he accompanied the Army to Halifax, and in June, to New York, where, states his biographer, he became 'the principal engineer in the army'. He accompanied Sir William Howe to

Philadelphia and in May 1778, on Howe's resignation as Commander-in-Chief, became the crony of Sir Henry Clinton, his successor. Montrésor returned to New York in June, and in the autumn of 1778 he sailed to England 'being in bad health from old wounds and various ailments'. Webster says:

> Of the many distinguished British officers who served in America during the eventful second half of the 18th century, it is doubtful if any had a more varied or more interesting experience than John Montrésor. He was a man of strong character and great determination, performing his duties with energy and enthusiasm. He had a keen and critical mind and his abilities were manifested in various directions. As a military engineer he stood in the highest rank. As a surveyor, he had a most extensive experience. His plans, maps, and drawings testify to his accomplishments as an artist.

Montrésor's retirement was marred by his fight for the redress of certain grievances arising from the Government's refusal to grant proper rank to engineer officers, and by the law-suits brought by the Treasury in respect to his accounts, some of which lacked vouchers. His estates were seized and sold. His sons cleared his name in 1826, obtaining £40,000 for the losses their father had suffered. The contemporary Loyalist historian, Thomas Jones (*History of New York During the Revolutionary War*, New York, 1897), accused Montrésor of having 'feathered his nest' from engineering contracts.

Des Barres's Journals have not survived, so we do not know if he landed on the island. I have compared Des Barres's drawing of Oak Island with a modern air-photograph having enlarged part of his chart to the same size. There are wide differences. Nonetheless this shore-line must have been drawn from personal inspection for many tiny indentations are shown. He indicates, but does not name, Smith's Cove and at its mouth the boulder in which the ring-bolt was found affixed in 1795. The 'Anchor' shown off shore suggests that he found a safe anchorage nearby. He shows no internal features.

Des Barres's life has been described by J. C. Webster (*The Life of Joseph Frederick Wallet Des Barres*. Privately printed. Shediac, New Brunswick, 1933). On the publication of his charts he claimed from the Admiralty and was finally paid thirty-five pounds for each of his 247 plates. This large sum, £8,645, failed to satisfy him. Due to his long service as a hydrographer, he had failed to achieve promotion to the army rank to which he was entitled and he demanded compensation, claiming £9,000. He retained his grievance, states Rear-Admiral G. S. Ritchie, Hydrographer of the Navy (*The Admiralty Chart*, 1967), who senses 'that it was the idea of some harassed official in Whitehall', to offer Des Barres the Governorship of Cape Breton and Prince Edward Islands. His career in this post was stormy. The Regimental History of the King's Royal Rifle Corps (The Royal American Regiment) of which he was an original member, states that Des Barres 'seems to have had an unfortunate propensity for quarrelling with everyone he met. Stories of his pugnacious character are still told in Nova Scotia.'

To celebrate his 100th birthday Des Barres danced on the dining table to amuse his friends. He died in Halifax in 1824 aged one hundred and two years.

A note prepared by the Admiralty Hydrographic Department and issued in connection with their leaflet, *Early Charts of the East Coast of North America*, describes Des Barres: 'In a century of great marine surveyors, the selfish, friendless, uncompromising Des Barres, for all his fault, stands pre-eminent. He lacked the exploring spirit of Cook, and the scholarly imagination of Dalrymple, but for skill and versatility as both a surveyor and a draughtsman, he had no equal. The accuracy of his charting, often carried out under conditions of imminent danger, is matched only by the delicacy and balance of his compilations.'

These surveys, and certainly the one made by Des Barres, would have been known to serving British military engineers, many of whom spent their entire careers in North America, where they may have learned to employ the word 'rock' for 'stone'. I have listed the names of thirty-five Royal Engineer officers, who served in North America between 1775 and 1782. We know little or nothing about them, other than their steps in promotion. During the war years, Captain William Spry was Chief Royal Engineer at Halifax. He employed his miners at the Citadel to dig a well 160 ft. deep, by the north wall of No. 18 Casement, and ran a conduit, large enough for a man, to connect with the drain into the harbour. (H. Piers.) He returned to England at the close of the war in 1782, and died in London in 1801 having attained the rank of Major-General.

A force of engineers could have reached Mahone Bay, either by land from Halifax, or by sea from there or from New York. The surveys made in 1762 and 1768 show a road or track skirting the bay's shores and leading to the town of Lunenburg, which had been settled in 1753 and used, in February 1755, by a party of Rangers led by Captain-Lieutenant Lewis. In the previous year Captain Ephraim Cook had established a block-house at the head of Mahone Bay, equipping it with twenty small guns.

The engineers could have employed the block-house on the Mush Mash river as a base and this may have required the building of a road across the island from the narrow and shallow channel dividing the island from the mainland. More probably they came by ship. The sea around Oak Island would have been navigable to small vessels such as transports, which were usually less than 200 tons. 'Mahone Bay is not fit for large ships,' states a Report made in 1761 (Appendix to H. Piers, *Evolution of the Halifax Fortress, 1749-1928*, 1947). *The Nova Scotia and Bay of Fundy Pilot*, Tenth Edition, 1958, states that the Oak Island area 'is not accessible without local knowledge'.

Two vessels were shown on 'Westhaver's chart', the 'treasure map', as we may call it. One was named the *Rose* and the other either the *Belmore* or *Balmore*. I attempted to trace ships bearing these names in about 1775-82; I searched at the British Museum and the Public Records Office; corresponding with the Shipping Editor, Lloyd's of London, the National Maritime Museum, the British Admiralty Library, the Library of Congress, and, remembering that tropical fibre had been found on the island, with the Institute of Jamaica; instigated research in the Custom House Records at Halifax, and in old Nova Scotian newspapers; read books dealing with the history of the British Navy and several about privateers and I found many contemporary journals relating to the war in America.

I traced a number of '*Roses*', but no vessel named '*Belmore*' or '*Balmore*' although several vessels carried similar names. I came across a storeship named *Belmont*, which was taken by the French in 1795, several ships named *Baltimore*,

136

and the Bristol privateer *Bellona.* J. W. D. Powell (*Bristol Privateers and Ships of War,* Bristol, 1930) supplies information about *Bellona.* Awarded Letters of Marque on 1 September 1779, the *Bellona.* Awarded during the next two years in the West Indies under the command of Captain James Hamilton Kennedy.

I found three British frigates named *Rose.* The first, a sixth rate, had been launched in 1740 and achieved considerable fame under Captain Thomas Franklin (W. E. Hay, '*Captain Franklin's Rose,*' *The American Neptune,* Vol. 26, 1926). Her Captain's Log, which I found at the Public Record Office, appeared to yield exciting information. In December 1744, the *Rose, 20* had taken, after a stubborn fight, the treasure-ship *Concepcion,* bound from Cartegna to Havana. I found a reference to the capture of the *Concepcion* in Sir Laird Clowes, *History of the Royal Navy,* (1901) Vol. IV: 'As she was not condemned by legal process, the exact value of her lading is unknown. It will be enough, however, to say that it consisted chiefly of gold, silver and jewels, and that such additional finds as "20,000" and "30,000" pistols made after the ships had been cleared, were looked upon by comparison as trifles.'

My speculation that Franklin may have kept quiet about the value of his prize, and hidden the lot on Oak Island, was dashed. His capture was too well known for such a clandestine operation. Captain Franklin's *Rose* was sold in 1757 and her name given to another twenty-four-gun frigate, 450 tons, built at Hull in 1757. This ship had a remarkable career during the Revolutionary War being actively engaged in the operation which resulted, in 1776, in the capture of New York, and she made several voyages including one to Halifax, Nova Scotia.

I found her Captain's Logs at the Public Record Office. Philip Brown became her Captain in December 1777. On 29 April 1779, at New York, he took on board THREE CHESTS OF TREASURE, containing £10,000 Sterling. The Log ended next day. Search revealed that there were no more 'Captain's Logs', but, her Master Thomas Chambers, had also kept a Log. The Admiralty Papers Catalogue disclosed that it covered the period from 25 February to 20 September 1779. This Log also recorded the reception on board of chests of treasure. On 7 May the *Rose* sailed from New York in convoy with several vessels. Would she turn north towards Nova Scotia?

She went south to Savannah, Georgia. On 22 May the 'Treasure' was taken ashore, for the payment of troops and the purchase of supplies. On 20 September the *Rose* was sunk to block the harbour against the French fleet.

In 1783 the name *Rose* was given to another frigate, twenty-eight guns, 593 tons. This *Rose* made several voyages from England to Newfoundland and Nova Scotia but her Captain's Logs noted nothing remarkable. She was wrecked on 28 June 1794 at Rocky Point, Jamaica.

These discoveries did not particularly disappoint me. I thought it unlikely that a frigate would have been permitted to sail into the shallows of Mahone Bay so I kept a look out for a smaller vessel named *Rose* and also searched for one bearing a name similar to *Belmore*.

During the course of writing my book dealing with the American Revolution, I read Major John André's *Journal* (edited C. de W. Willcox, Tarrytown, New York, 1930). André was the unfortunate British officer who was executed as a spy in 1780. He mentions the presence of a small transport named *Rose*, and another named *John and Bella*, 194 tons, at New York in August 1778. Admiral Thomas Graves (*The Graves Papers*, Publications of the Naval History Society, VII, New York, 1916) referred to a transport and victualler named *Bellona*, Master, Thomas Waddell. She was taken by the Americans in the York River on 9 November 1781.

These entries disclosed that, about 1779, two small transports, the *Rose* and the *Bellona*, were stationed in American waters. Whether or not the *Bellona* was one of the vessels engaged, their small tonnage would have enabled them to navigate the intricacies of Mahone Bay. The British Military Engineers used small transports when they needed to move by sea. No strong conclusions can be drawn from the existence of ships of similar names to those shown on Westhaver's chart.

Why did the British Engineers, or anyone else for that matter, choose Oak Island upon which to make a concealment? The answer lies, apparently, in its geological formation. Mahone Bay forms part of a 'drumlin', low, gently sloping ground, moulded by the last ice-sheet, which left layers of deposit. Thus, unlike most of Nova Scotia which is rocky, Oak Island is composed of soil to considerable depth. A competent surveyor or engineer, but hardly a pirate, would have inferred that a deep shaft could be dug there without reaching rock.

I have tried to find a reasonable alternative to the belief that the Oak Island works were constructed to form a concealment.

Could the military engineers have been doing something else, carrying out a test or experiment? I racked my brains to find an alternative, however improbable. It is possible that they could have been testing a method for bringing water within a beleaguered fort: it is built adjacent to river or lake; its garrison expecting to be besieged, dig a tunnel downwards from the water supply, and excavate a well within the fort. Extravagant as this idea may be, I found proof that such a ruse had been employed by the British during the Revolutionary War.

In 1781, the small British post at Fort Watson on the Santee River, South Carolina, was besieged by an American force led by Colonels Henry Lee and Francis Marion. The garrison of 120 men was commanded by Lieutenant McKay. He occupied a stockaded fort built on an old Indian mound close to the river. (H. Lee, *Memoirs of the War in the Southern Department*, New York, 1872, and W. G. Sims, *Francis Marion*, New York, 1844.)

McKay faced inevitable defeat unless he could devise some means of procuring water. According to Lee, he 'cut a trench' from the nearby river to his fosse and Marion says that the besieged garrison sank a well 'within the stockade, below the level of the contiguous water'. The Americans countered McKay's ruse. During the night they built a wooden tower which overlooked the fort and at dawn their marksmen swept the stockades with fire. McKay was forced to capitulate.

No large-scale map exists of Fort Watson, which is due for archaeological exploration as I was told by the South Carolina Department of Archives and History. The South Carolina Historical Society also replied to my query.

This use of a trench as a means of bringing water into a shaft is no proof that the British military engineers tested such a method. Why would they do so on an island, and with sea-water?

McKay's stratagem at Fort Watson gives rise to other

speculations. Did the British adopt what may have been an ancient American practice, employed perhaps in frontier forts? Such an idea may have been the inspiration behind the Money Pit defences.

The design whereby a shaft becomes flooded upon re-excavation thus blocking access to its depths, seems unique to Oak Island. Perhaps the concept belonged to Mr X alone.

The man who conceived the idea of making an impregnable concealment, by harnessing the tides, or who put it into execution, was in all probability a British military engineer. Either he, or the naval officer concerned in the operation, noted the directions for the recovery of the deposit on a chart. This chart was either based on, or may have been a section cut from, Des Barres's chart which is described as 'Published for the use of the Royal Navy of Great Britain'. It is possible to carry the identification further. Mr X, or his naval collaborator, used a particular copy of Des Barres's chart. The 'treasure-map', the chart carrying the directions, also bore the puzzling letters 'H.S.O.H.E.' Colonel F. F. Stear, Secretary and Librarian of the Royal Engineer Historical Society, supplied the solution to their meaning in: HYDRO-GRAPHIC SURVEY OFFICE(R) HALIFAX ESTABLISHMENT. The use of such a title, and its abbreviation, would have been normal eighteenth-century 'service' practice. William Spry, and his predecessors and successors, for example, described themselves as C R E HALIFAX – CHIEF ROYAL ENGINEER.

Whether or not the Halifax engineers instituted the work on the island, they were concerned in the job. The impetus, however, may have come from New York, the British command post in North America.

I studied the history of the war with the rebel colonists to find a reference to, or reason for, a concealment such as that on Oak Island. I searched through the Military, Naval and Colonial Office papers preserved at the Public Records Office, London, and I enquired at the W. L. Clements Library, the University of Michigan, where the 'British Head-quarters Papers' of the period are kept. So far I have failed to find any order or report concerning the operation. That may not be surprising since officers in those days did not often commit themselves to paper – verbal orders and reports usually sufficing – and the operation was in all probability a clandestine affair, demanding secrecy.

Had the British needed to make a concealment, the Commander-in-Chief in North America would have made the decision. Thomas Gage was succeeded early in 1776 by Sir William Howe who, in turn, gave way in May 1778 to Sir Henry Clinton. Sir Guy Carleton, later Lord Dorchester, the Commander at Montreal, came to New York and took over from Clinton in 1782 at the end of the war. Clinton was thus in charge between 1778 and 1782, the years in question.

In the summer of 1778, New York was threatened by Washington's Army and the French fleet. As early as 21 March, the Secretary of State for the Colonies, Lord George Germain, had authorized the evacuation of the city if its garrison was in danger. (Instructions to Sir Henry Clinton for the Conduct of the Campaign in North America 1778-82, P.R.O., c/o 5/263.) If the worst came, Clinton could fall back on Halifax. On 29 July, Clinton warned Germain that he 'might be compelled to evacuate the city and return to Halifax'. He expected to use 'the discretion given to me' before the end of September. The crisis dissolved when the French fleet was scattered in a storm.

Could Clinton, fearing the hazards of sudden flight, and a blockade of Halifax, have sought to safeguard his 'sinews of war', the military chest? Large sums in specie were sent from London for the payment of troops and the purchase of supplies. On 25 June 1776, for example, the Deputy Paymaster-General received £840,776 from the Treasury. During the winter of 1778-9 the chest was low. Between 1770 and 1783 £17,002,598 was supplied to the armies in North America by the contract with the bankers, Harley and Drummond. Clinton may have ordered the engineers to conceal part of the gold on the small island in Mahone Bay, recommended possibly by his crony, John Montrésor. This theory carries an obvious corollary: the gold must have been recovered. If Clinton had failed to account for a large sum of money he would have been hounded by the Treasury to the end of his days. The scandal would have been prodigious.

It is possible that the work was done by the Royal Engineers on their own initiative. They were part, not of the army, but of the Ordnance Board, a separate service, and were independent of military control. The Board of Ordnance controlled their own shipping, owning several small transports and other vessels in American waters.

I 'reconstruct' the possible course of events thus. Alarmed by the threat to the army's 'security', posed by the entry of France into what had previously been a domestic quarrel, the Commander-in-Chief decided it would be advisable to conceal a large sum of money in a place of both absolute safety and ease of access. He called in his engineers. An officer outlined his plan whereby the deposit could be protected by the combination of air and water pressure. His Grand Design would have impressed his General, just as it has fascinated us in retrospect. Given the 'go-ahead', the engineers put it in execution, possibly with the assistance of the miners stationed in Halifax. The money would have been transferred from New York to Mahone Bay by ship, and its movement would probably have been delayed until the engineers reported that the place of concealment was prepared.

What is the final solution of the puzzle? It seems to depend upon the discovery of a document which may not exist and may not have been written. I doubt if excavation alone will solve the mystery.

Perhaps Triton will penetrate to the cavity at 212 ft. They may find something sensational, but in all probability not significant. A workman employed by the original depositors may have fallen accidentally into a solution cavern, due to the collapse of the lower flood tunnel. No one, in my opinion, would have placed treasure in a cavity at that depth, in a treacherous area susceptible to flooding, from where it could not be recovered.

I believe the spots chosen by Johnson and me hold greater promise. If the directions and code mean anything they seem to indicate positions on the surface below which caches were made. Why, otherwise, were they devised and recorded? Neither place shows any evidence of re-excavation.

One day, I hope to excavate my spot at small cost. Whether or not I find anything, I only regret that I have failed to identify Mr X. He was a remarkable genius for, apparently, he did not boast of his exploit. Some disappointed treasure seekers have called him the greatest practical joker of all time. He has provided us with a tantalizing intriguing mystery about which many have speculated, as I have for more than thirty years.

Maybe a great treasure does lie in the soil of Oak Island? Like Everest it is 'there', a challenge to the human spirit. Can we defeat the Genius who nonchalantly left the old oak tree standing enticing us to dig below? I rather doubt it. In a sense I hope we never shall.

Postscript

Since this book was completed, I learned three additional pieces of information:

1. It was reported in the Halifax *Chronicle Herald*, 7 December 1971, that in August a team of divers had been lowered 235 ft. into a vast chamber or cavern which extended beneath the area of the Money Pit. One diver, Phil Irwin, told the reporter that he could not see any walls, only a ghostly ceiling having eight or ten '40 foot or more V shaped gouges' extending upward. Reflection of his light on the ceiling in certain spots resembled a fluorescent light. He could not see bottom (through the water) but stood on it. The descent shaft was protected down to 180 ft. by a 26 in. metal pipe, and continued through bedrock to about 225 ft. At about 180 ft. water rushed in so fast that it was sweeping the mask from the diver's face. The flow of water was stopped when Mr Blakenship, Triton's field manager, bulldozed soil into the sea where it was thought the entrance to the flood tunnel was located. Drilling passed through a 2½ ft. flood tunnel at the 212 ft. level. Beach rocks had been used in its construction.

(Nothing, apparently, was found to confirm or deny the conclusions drawn from the television photographs previously obtained in the cavity at 212 ft. depth. It was not stated whether the shaft drilled for the divers was at the same spot, or where these shafts were in relation to the Money Pit. This new information appears to disclose the existence of a large cavern, possibly a geological phenomenon, beneath the eastern end of the island. It appears to be connected to the beach by one or more man-made tunnels.)

2. Mr P. J. Mallon, of 'Ivanhoe', Saint Field Road, Carryduff, Belfast, Northern Ireland (as he told me on the telephone), visited Oak Island in March 1972. On 20 March he found a stone triangle on the south shore, approximately 480 ft. south-east of the Money Pit. This is a different triangle to that found in 1937 by Roper and Hedden. Its dimensions are similar, but the 'Mallon' triangle lacks the

half circle of stones which encompass the base of the Hedden triangle. The Mallon triangle points north and thus may indicate the Cave-In shaft, about 470 ft. distant. (The ground in between, it needs to be remarked, rises and is obscured by trees.) The triangle, Mallon told me, was completely obscured and covered by moss. He found it because he expected to find such a triangle at that spot. He believes that there may be others like it on the island. He based his expectation on his knowledge of ancient Irish 'shore-land' drainage systems, where the 'sluice-gates', in the drains, were marked by triangles or stone arrows. Mr Mallon believes that such 'sluice' or water gates exist on the island and await discovery; by them the flow of water into the Money Pit can be stopped.

No such water gates have ever been found. It is curious, however, that the Mallon triangle points apparently at the Cave-In shaft. That shaft and the surrounding area was deeply excavated in 1965 without disclosing the existence of any 'water-gate'.

Mallon's triangle, on the other hand, may have been intended to indicate, as a 'cross-reference', the site of the Cave-In shaft, to which I attach significance as possibly the site of the treasure cache.

3. In the late nineteen thirties, a family named Adams lived on the island, where they were employed as caretakers. Their daughter, Peggy, was aged about four, had not been to school and had not seen a book. One winter day she came running to her mother saying she had seen 'many men wearing red coats and hats looking like firemen's helmets'. Her mother went with Peggy to the place, somewhere between Smith's Cove and the Money Pit. There were no footmarks in the snow. Some years later, Mrs Adams took Peggy to the Citadel at Halifax, which houses a museum. It contains (as I have seen) effigies of British soldiers dressed in the uniforms of the period 1754-1783. The hats are not unlike 'fireman's helmets'. 'Those are the men I saw,' exclaimed Peggy. (Nothing, of course, can be made of this story. It is possible that the human mind contains a mechanism which enables some individuals to see back in time.)

Bibliography

AKINS, T. B. *History of Halifax City* (Nova Scotia Hist. Soc. VII) 1895

ALLEN, G. W. *Massachusetts' Privateers* 1927

ALLISON, D. *History of Nova Scotia*, 3 vols. 1916

ANDRE, John *Journal – Operations of the British Army, June 1777 to November, 1778* Ed. C. de W. Willcox, Tarrytown, New York 1930

BLAIR, Frederick *Records of Oak Island*, loaned by his son, Gordon Blair

BLEAKNEY, J. Sherman *Reports of Marine Turtles from New England and Eastern Canada*, Canadian Field Naturalist, vol. 7 No. 2 June 1965

BOWDOIN, H. L. *Solving the Mystery of Oak Island*. Collier's Magazine, 18 August 1911

BREBNER, J. B. *New England's Outpost* 1927, *Neutral Yankees of Nova Scotia* 1937

BRIGGS, Henry *A Brief History of Mine Surveying* Historical Review of Coal Mining 1925

BRISAY, Mather Des *History of Lunenburg County* 1870

BRYMNER, D. *Calendar of Nova Scotia State Papers* (1603-1801) 1894

CAMPBELL, G. G. *History of Nova Scotia* 1948

Colonist, The 2, 5, 7 January 1864

CONNOLLY, T. W. J. *History of the Sappers and Miners*, 2 vols. 1857

Corpus Christi (Texas) *Caller*, 29 September and 28 October 1955

DAWSON, E. and DALGETHY, L. C. *The March of the Compass in Canada* Canadian Surveyor, vol. XXI, No. 5 December 1967

DES BARRES, J. F. W. *The Atlantic Neptune* 4 vols. 1779-81

DRISCOLL, C. B. *Doubloons* 1931

FARIBAULT, E. R. *Summary Report* Geological Survey, N.S. Dep. of Mines 1911

FREDEA, Josephine Article on 'Oak Island' *Collier's Magazine*, 23 September 1905

GRAVES, Admiral Thomas *Papers*, Naval Hist. Soc. VII. (ed. F. E. Chadwick) N.Y. 1916

HALIBURTON, T. C. *Historical and Statistical Account of Nova Scotia*. 2 vols. 1829

Halifax *Herald Chronicle* Oak Island File

HAMILTON, P. S. *Oak Island* Enterprise, New Glasgow February, March, April 1894

HARING, G. H. *The Buccaneers in The West Indies in the XVII Century* London 1910
Trade and Navigation Between Spain and the Indies in the Time of the Hapsburgs Harvard U.P. 1918

HARRIS, R. V. *The Oak Island Mystery* Toronto 1958

Historical Manuscripts Commission. *Report on American Manuscripts in the Royal Institution* vols. I and III 1904-9

HOWE, E. H. and HURWITZ, L. *Magnetic Surveys* U.S. Gov. Printing Office 1964

HOWLETT, A. *The Mystery of Captain Kidd's Treasure* World Wide Magazine, October 1958

KERR, W. B. *The Marine Provinces and the American Revolution* 1942

KILBRACKEN, Lord *Morgan's Gold* London *Evening Standard*, 8/12 March 1957

LEARY, T. P. *The Oak Island Enigma*, Omaha, Nebraska 1953

LINGEL, R. *The Atlantic Neptune*, N.Y. Public Library Bulletin vol. 40 No. 7 1936

MAY, W. E. *'Captain Franklin's Rose', The American Neptune*, vol. 26 1926

MCLENNAN, J. S. *Louisbourg from its Foundation to its Fall, 1715-1758* 1918

Mines, Canadian Dept. of *Geological Survey* 1929

MORRELL, Parker *The Money Pit* Saturday Evening Post, 14 October 1939

MURDOCK, Beamish *History of Nova Scotia*, 3 vols. 1865

Nova Scotia, Dept. of Mines *Stratigraphy of the Windsor Group.* 1954; *Gypsum and Andyrite in N.S.* 1952

OBER, Frederick *Islands of the Caribbean* N.Y. 1904

PIERS, Henry *Evolution of the Halifax Fortress 1749-1928* Public Archives Nova Scotia. 1947

PORTER, Whitworth Watson *History of the Corps of Engineers.* 1889-1913

POWELL, J. W. B. *Bristol Privateers and Ships of War.* 1930

RANDALL, T. *Halifax, Warden of the North.* 1948

RICHIE, R. S. *The Admiralty Chart* 1967

SCULL, G. D. *John Montrésor Journals* N.Y. Hist. Soc. Collections for 1881, 1882

SHORT, D. and DOUGHTY, A. G. *Canada and its Provinces*, vol. XIII. 1913

SLOANE, Sir Hans *Natural History of Jamaica* vol. II. 1725

SNOW, E. R. *Mysteries and Adventures Along the Atlantic Coast* N.Y. 1948

SPEDON, A. I. *Rambles Among the Blue Noses* 1863

STEVENS, Henry, Son & Stiles *Notes Biographical and Bibliographical on the Atlantic Neptune* 1937

SYRETT, David *Shipping and the American War 1775-83* University of London Historical Studies No. XXVII. 1970

WALTON, Alarik Diagrams and Notes, Map Room, British Museum 1960

WEBSTER, J. C. *The Life of John Montrésor*, Trans. Royal Soc. of Canada, Series 111, vol. XXII. 1928

Joseph Frederick Wallet Des Barres Shediac, New Brunswick 1933

WENTWORTH, H. *American Dialect Dictionary* 1944

WILKINS, H. T. *Treasure Hunting* 1932; *Captain Kidd's Skeleton Island* 1935; *A Modern Treasure Hunter* 1948

WILLCOX, W. B. *The American Rebellion. Sir Henry Clinton's Narratives, 1775-82* New Haven 1954

Portrait of a General: Sir Henry Clinton New York 1964

MAHONE BAY CHARTS: U.S. Navy Nautical Chart No.: 5506

Royal Canadian Navy Nautical Chart No.: 4381

British Admiralty Nautical Chart No.: 730

Appendices

A British Military Engineer Officers serving in North America 1775-82

BARRON Edward
BENDYSKE Richard
BLASKOWITCH Charles

CAMBEL John
CAMPBELL Archibald
COUTINE Peter

DEBBEIG Hugh
DIXON Matthew
DURNFORD Alexander

GARTH George
GLENNIS James
GORDON Harry

HALDANE Henry
HARTCUP Thomas
HYDE-PAGE Thomas William

KERSTEMAN William

MARR John

MERCER Alexander
MIST Charles
MONCRIEFF James
MONTRESOR John
MORSE Robert
MULCASTER Frederick George

PARKER William
PHILIPS
(with assist – Calbeck)
PITTS Matthew

RUDYARD Thomas

SKINNER William Campbell
SLACK Benjamin
SPRY William
STRATTON John
SUTHERLAND Alexander

TWISS...
TYERS William

WADE John

B Various Shafts

In all, twenty-one shafts have been sunk by various searchers. The position of many is uncertain.
I list their likely position from the information available.

1			The original shaft (The Money Pit).
2	1805	110 ft.	14 ft. east of Money Pit.
3	1850	109 ft.	10 ft. NW of Money Pit.
4	1850 to	75 ft.	near beach, Smith's Cove.
5	1850 to	35 ft.	12 ft. to south of Money Pit.
6	1850 to	118 ft.	50 ft. south of Money Pit.
7	1863 to	107 ft.	west and close to Money Pit.
8	1863	?	close to No. 6.
9	1863 to	120 ft.	100 ft. south-east of Money Pit.
10	1866	?	175 ft. south of flood-tunnel.
11	1894 to	52 ft.	the Cave-In shaft.
12	1894 to	55 ft.	8 ft. north and 30 ft. east of Money Pit.
13	1894	?	probably a few feet north of Cave-In shaft.
14	1897 to	112 ft.	somewhere south-west of Money Pit.
15	1898 to	168 ft.	80 ft. south-west of Money Pit.

16 ⎫
17 ⎪ 1898/9? probably south-east of Money Pit
18 ⎬   (but No. 16 could have been to its north-
19 ⎭   west.)

20		? to 113 ft.	west of Money Pit.
21	1931	?	Chappell Shaft (south-west corner of Money Pit).
22	1937	?	Hedden Shaft (south-east corner of Money Pit).

Dunfield Excavations
1965	80 ft. wide to 130 ft.	Money Pit.
	80 ft. wide to 100 ft.	Cave-In.
	100 ft. long to 50 ft.	Triangle.

C   Treasure Trove Act CHAPTER 314

REVISED STATUTES OF NOVA SCOTIA 1967. Queen's Printer, Halifax, Nova Scotia 1967

1   The Governor in Council may from time to time by license under the hand of the Provisional Secretary grant to any person the right to search in any part of the Province specified in the license for precious stones or metals in a state other than their natural state and to recover and retain the same upon the payment to the Provincial Secretary of a royalty thereon at such rate as the Governor in Council may prescribe, RS, c.299, S.I.

2   The Governor in Council may prescribe the terms and conditions of any such license and upon being satisfied that there

has been breach of or failure to perform those terms or conditions or any of them by the licensee he may cancel the license. RS, c.299, s.2.

3 No such license shall be transferred or assigned without the written permission of the Provincial Secretary. RS, c.299, s.3.

4 When any person whether the holder of a license issued under this Act or not discovers or recovers any precious stones or metals in a state other than their natural state or any treasure or treasure trove he shall forthwith make a report in writing verified upon oath to the Provincial Secretary setting out full particulars of the articles, treasure or treasure trove so discovered or recovered, the location of the discovery and the place at which the said articles, treasure or treasure trove may be inspected by the Provincial Secretary or by some person on his behalf. RS, c.299, s.4.

5 The Provincial Secretary may upon payment of a royalty at the rate prescribed by a license confirm to the holder of a license the right to retain for his own use and benefit any precious metals or stones in a state other than their natural state and any treasure and treasure trove discovered and recovered by him within the area covered by his license. RS, c.299, s.5.

6 The holder of a license issued under this Act may in accordance with the terms and conditions of his license enter and search upon Crown Lands within the area covered by the license. RS, c.299, s.6.

7 No holder of a license shall enter or search upon private lands except with the consent of the owner, tenant or occupant thereof or under special license from the Provincial Secretary. RS, c. 299, s.7.

8

(1) The holder of a license who is unable to make an agreement with the owner, tenant or occupant of private lands for the right to enter and search upon private lands within the area covered by his license may apply to the Provincial Secretary, after notice to the owner, tenant or occupant, for a special license to enter and search upon such lands.

(2) The Provincial Secretary after hearing the parties may grant such special license upon such terms and conditions as he may think proper, and may determine the amount of compensation to be paid to such owner, tenant or occupant and the manner and time of payment of the same.

(3) The Provincial Secretary may order the giving of security for payment of the compensation and may prohibit, pending the determination of the proceedings or until the compensation is paid or secured, further entry or search by such licensee or any person claiming under him.

(4) Where there are several owners, tenants or occupants of the lands sought to be entered and there are, in the opinion of the Provincial Secretary, special difficulties in effecting service of any notice under this Section, he may order substituted service in such manner as he may determine.

(5) There shall be no appeal from the granting by the Provincial Secretary of such special license nor from any order for security nor from any order or decision or ruling in respect thereto.

(6) A licensee or other person aggrieved by the determination by the Provincial Secretary pursuant to this Section of the amount of compensation may, within thirty days of that determination, appeal therefrom to the county court of the district in which the land lies, and, on such appeal, that court may determine the amount of compensation to be paid by the licensee. RS, c.299, s.8.

9

(1) When the holder of a license issued under Section I requires any land within the area covered by his license or any right or interest therein for the purpose of entering and searching upon and recovering precious stones or metals in other than their natural state or any treasure or treasure trove and he is unable to acquire such land, right or interest by agreement with the owner he may proceed by way of petition to the Provincial Secretary in the same manner as a lessee under the Mines Act may proceed by petition to the Minister of Mines under Section 111 of the Mines Act.

(2) Sections 111 to 116 inclusive of the Mines Act shall apply *mutatis mutandis* to proceedings under this Section and the Provincial Secretary shall have and may exercise with respect to any lands covered by a license issued under Section 1 all the power and authority that the Minister of Mines has with respect to lands within the limits of a mining lease. RS, c.299 s.9.

D   Ancient Units of Measure

1 ROD=5½ yards or 16½ feet
1 CHAIN=22 yards or 66 feet

Index

A Fontana Selection

Famous Animal Books in Fontana

JOY ADAMSON
Born Free (illus.)   **Living Free** (illus.)
Forever Free (illus.)

GERALD DURRELL
Birds, Beasts and Relatives   **Two in the Bush**
Fillets of Plaice   **Catch Me a Colobus**
Rosy is My Relative   (illus.)

JACQUIE DURRELL
Beasts in My Bed (illus.)

JANE VAN LAWICK GOODALL
In the Shadow of Man (illus.)

B. and M. GRZIMEK
Serengeti Shall Not Die (illus.)

BUSTER LLOYD-JONES
The Animals Came in One by One
Come into My World
Love on a Lead (illus.)

EVE PALMER
The Plains of Camdeboo (illus.)